T0079684

BEANS

Edible

Series Editor: Andrew F. Smith

EDIBLE is a revolutionary series of books dedicated to food and drink that explores the rich history of cuisine. Each book reveals the global history and culture of one type of food or beverage.

Already published

Apple Erika Janik, *Avocado* Jeff Miller, *Banana* Lorna Piatti-Farnell, *Barbecue* Jonathan Deutsch and Megan J. Elias, *Beans* Natalie Rachel Morris, *Beef* Lorna Piatti-Farnell, *Beer* Gavin D. Smith, *Berries* Heather Arndt Anderson, *Biscuits and Cookies* Anastasia Edwards, *Brandy* Becky Sue Epstein, *Bread* William Rubel, *Cabbage* Meg Muckenhoupt, *Cake* Nicola Humble, *Caviar* Nichola Fletcher, *Champagne* Becky Sue Epstein, *Cheese* Andrew Dalby, *Chillies* Heather Arndt Anderson, *Chocolate* Sarah Moss and Alexander Badenoch, *Cocktails* Joseph M. Carlin, *Coffee* Jonathan Morris, *Corn* Michael Owen Jones, *Curry* Colleen Taylor Sen, *Dates* Nawal Nasrallah, *Doughnut* Heather Delancey Hunwick, *Dumplings* Barbara Gallani, *Edible Flowers* Constance L. Kirker and Mary Newman, *Eggs* Diane Toops, *Fats* Michelle Phillipov, *Figs* David C. Sutton, *Game* Paula Young Lee, *Gin* Lesley Jacobs Solmonson, *Hamburger* Andrew F. Smith, *Herbs* Gary Allen, *Herring* Kathy Hunt, *Honey* Lucy M. Long, *Hot Dog* Bruce Kraig, *Ice Cream* Laura B. Weiss, *Lamb* Brian Yarvin, *Lemon* Toby Sonneman, *Lobster* Elisabeth Townsend, *Melon* Sylvia Lovegren, *Milk* Hannah Velten, *Moonshine* Kevin R. Kosar *Mushroom* Cynthia D. Bertelsen, *Mustard* Demet Güzey, *Nuts* Ken Albala, *Offal* Nina Edwards, *Olive* Fabrizia Lanza, *Onions and Garlic* Martha Jay, *Oranges* Clarissa Hyman, *Oyster* Carolyn Tillie, *Pancake* Ken Albala, *Pasta and Noodles* Kantha Shelke, *Pickles* Jan Davison, *Pie* Janet Clarkson *Pineapple* Kaori O'Connor, *Pizza* Carol Helstosky, *Pomegranate* Damien Stone, *Pork* Katharine M. Rogers, *Potato* Andrew F. Smith, *Pudding* Jeri Quinzio, *Rice* Renee Marton, *Rum* Richard Foss, *Salad* Judith Weinraub, *Salmon* Nicolaas Mink, *Sandwich* Bee Wilson, *Sauces* Maryann Tebben, *Sausage* Gary Allen, *Seaweed* Kaori O'Connor, *Shrimp* Yvette Florio Lane, *Soup* Janet Clarkson, *Spices* Fred Czarra, *Sugar* Andrew F. Smith, *Sweets and Candy* Laura Mason, *Tea* Helen Saberi, *Tequila* Ian Williams, *Tomato* Clarissa Hyman, *Truffle* Zachary Nowak, *Vodka* Patricia Herlihy, *Water* Ian Miller, *Whiskey* Kevin R. Kosar, *Wine* Marc Millon

Beans

A Global History

Natalie Rachel Morris

REAKTION BOOKS

*This is for the women of my life: those who've raised me,
mentored me, stood by my side. Together, we rise.*

Published by Reaktion Books Ltd
Unit 32, Waterside
44–48 Wharf Road
London N1 7UX, UK
www.reaktionbooks.co.uk

First published 2020
Copyright © Natalie Rachel Morris 2020

Printed and bound in India by Replika Press Pvt. Ltd

A catalogue record for this book is available from the British Library

ISBN 978 1 78914 204 4

Contents

Introduction

The story of beans is the age-old narrative of the underdog. In their earliest forms, beans gave our hunter-gatherer ancestors a naturally sweet and crunchy snack that would have been satisfying and satiating during a time in which fire and cooking had yet to be discovered. Our relatives in pre-history knew an honest, laborious life where they shared responsibilities and survival was their priority.

As the world advanced, so did social structure, hierarchy and class. Lentils, favas and garbanzos were among the first beans known to exist and as such were some of the first foods to carry social significance. As cooking facilities became available, beans were abandoned by the rich in favour of meat and left as food for the poor. In Imperial Rome, lentils were an ancient form of packing peanuts, providing a cushion for the Vatican Obelisk as it travelled from Egypt to its new home.

Seen as taboo, beans had more than just meat stacked against them. Early influencers like Pythagoras, the vegetarian geometer, outwardly avoided beans. An apparently close encounter in a bean field led him to ban bean-eating (and bean fields) among his followers. Biblical literature tells us that it was a bowl of lentils for which Esau sold his birthright, inciting an epic family drama. It was often believed that beans were

Colourful varieties of bulk beans at a market.

not only difficult to digest but suppressed sexual urges and were even the cause of leprosy. And lest we forget, 'digestive wind', an early euphemism for – you guessed it – flatulence, has blemished beans' reputation since their beginning.

Though today the hearsay narrative has generally been scientifically rectified, beans remain an unsung staple of diets worldwide, tucked into a taco or quietly adding substance to a stew. When people spread the all-American favourite peanut butter, whether crunchy or creamy, across their all-American white bread, most fail to recognize they are savouring a legume. Misunderstood, most beans are not only adding the popular twenty-first-century fad diet favourite of protein to a person's daily diet but are contributing high amounts of fibre and carbohydrates – minus the cholesterol and fat calories that can come with meat.

Perhaps most importantly, this dark horse hasn't seen the credit due for undoubtedly its greatest gift to all of humanity: nitrogen. It wasn't until recent years that natural nitrogen sources – legumes as cover crops – were removed from farming and agriculture. Planting them to feed the soil had been a common practice, reputedly dating almost as far back as the beginning of organized farming itself. It wasn't until their widespread removal after the Second World War that our present-day society began to understand beans' most valuable asset.

Among the barrage of inconsistent, unreliable and even downright ridiculous nutritional information and recommendations for ways to eat it, the humble bean has found its way

A bowl full of beans of Italian origin.

The neon 'beans bunny sign' in Saginaw Valley, Michigan, is the largest figural neon sign in the United States. Built in 1948, it helped to promote and sell stuffed bunnies that each represented a different bean grown in the area.

throughout history. Though its true identity is continually mistaken, it has fought through stigmas to earn its place as a sleeper candidate for the role of one of the most important food sources in history.

I

Bean Botany

In order to think about beans, we first need to learn about the larger legume family. All beans are legumes, but not all legumes are beans. One of the largest families, at 17,000 species,[1] the Leguminosae family includes vegetables such as beans, peas and lentils, feed crops like clover, and weeds like vetch. Today, it is more commonly known as the Fabaceae family. The common trait among these plants is the seedpod.

'Legume' is said to be derived from the Latin word *leger*, meaning 'to gather', since more than one seed could be harvested at a time. Always a single chamber, the pod can contain several seeds, each of which is composed of a large embryo and a little endosperm. In the case of the Fabaceae family, each seed is either a bean, pea or lentil and can either be eaten or saved for future planting.

Depending on where you are in the world, a bean, pea or lentil might simply be referred to more broadly as a legume. This holds true for most regions, but some places choose to refer specifically to a bean, pea or lentil instead. This book discusses beans specifically but cannot tell their story without a wider reference to their sister plants, whether they are peas, lentils or lesser-known legumes.

Mistaken Identity

Green beans, dry beans and canned beans. Pulses, peanuts and groundnuts. Clover, alfalfa, vanilla and fenugreek. With so many species of plants labelled as beans, and many of them mislabelled, how do we know which actually belong in this book?

The Old English word 'bean' derives from the Proto-Germanic word *bauno*, related to the Latin *faba*. Eaten since the beginning of recorded history, green beans are simply the fresh and raw (or 'green') versions of today's more commonly used canned and dried beans. Though the name 'green bean' conveniently refers to colour, it is nodding more towards youthfulness and, more often than not, the green bean's identity as a crunchy sweet vegetable that can be shades of any colour, depending on the variety. Though beans are most often eaten shelled (separated from their pods) the immaturity of an unshelled green bean allows it to be tender enough to eat pod and all. Pulses became the name for the dried version of legumes; the practice of canning would come in the late nineteenth century.

Falling within the Fabaceae family is a popular genus of beans primarily hailing from the New World, *Phaseolus*. This includes the four most commonly used varieties of bean: pinto, navy, kidney and black. *Phaseolus vulgaris* is also called the common bean, perhaps because it includes the afore-mentioned varieties that have become the suggested sides and fillers in nutritional mass marketing. But *P. vulgaris* is home to colourful, speckled, dotted, shapely and seeing-eye beans that have historic significance too. Often referred to as heirloom beans, these are all either pole or bush beans and include varieties like the stark black turtle bean, the pink-brush-stroked borlotti or cranberry bean, the tender and tiny

Peanuts are part of the Fabaceae family.

French flageolet and the nearly perfectly round half-black and half-pearly-white Calypso.

Named for the Anasazi natives of the American southwest, Anasazi beans were discovered in abandoned ancient dwellings in the late 1900s by researchers from the University of California, Los Angeles. The red and white bean had been naturally preserved over time, after having been closed in a clay pot and sealed with pine tar. The UCLA scientists were able to carbon date the beans to 500 BCE and germinate some for further conservation. Today, they are mainly cultivated in Arizona and are trademarked by Adobe Milling. Despite this commercialization, the Hopi, who are direct descendants of the Anasazi, still rely on them as a mainstay in their diet and use them as a symbol in their 'Powamuya' bean dance.

Hannibal Lecter may have preferred fava (broad) beans, but Hannibal the Carthaginian military general may have had a taste of one of the rarest *P. vulgaris* during his invasion of the Roman Republic. Still in existence, the hard-to-find fagiolina is known to grow exclusively near the area of Tuscany where he and his men staked their claim. People familiar with the Italian-based worldwide organization Slow Food might recognize the zolfino, a product of the non-profit's Ark of Taste programme that works to catalogue and ultimately

Fresh green and wax beans.

preserve rare and nearly extinct foods by way of educational promotional efforts. It has worked in the case of the zolfino; the buttery, yellow bean from the region of Pratomagno nearly vanished but is now commonly grown, sold and consumed, at least among Italians and Slow Food purists. The same can be said for other beans of Italian origin, including lamon and sorana. Though not registered in the Ark of Taste, they are safeguarded under the country's own protection plan, which acts in a similar fashion and even throws bean festivals in their places of origin.

France is no stranger to festivals for beans, either. They too celebrate heirloom varieties of New World beans, registering some of them under their country's own version of the protection plan, which includes a 'Label Rouge' for added quality control and legal distinction. The petite French flageolet is simply showcased next to a leg of lamb and, for those that love a good cassoulet, the haricot tarbais should be used. Best grown at the base of the Pyrenees, a bag of tarbais is even rumoured to have been gifted to Catherine de' Medici by her brother as a wedding gift when she arrived in Marseille in 1533.

The next two *Phaseolus* varieties seem to pit the big bean against the small, but balance one another out in terms of their strengths. *Phaseolus lunatus* are bigger beans, such as limas (sometimes referred to as butter beans) from Peru. Despite their size, most of these beans do not take any longer to cook than their smaller counterparts, and result in a creamy texture. Some have associated lima beans with a vegetal, bitter taste, which has resulted in the bean getting a bad reputation. But not the author of *Uncle Tom's Cabin*, Harriet Beecher Stowe, and her sister Catherine E. Beecher, who wrote a guide to household management. *The American Woman's Home* couldn't praise lima beans enough.

Cranberry beans are a new world staple.

All *P. lunatus* legumes hail from South America, while *Phaseolus acutifolius* originate from central and North America, specifically in what is now the southwest United States. The tiny tepary bean dominates this genus, but their small size is no indication of their environmental assets. Best cultivated in their native arid climate, they can be grown with little water and are found in hundreds of heritage varieties. Just like their cousins from the *vulgaris* variety, while most people might find the typical brown or white being sold on store shelves, the tepary bean also shows itself off in other colours and prints.

Phaseolus coccineus might be the one that onlookers are always smitten by. With their swinging branches and colourful pods and flowers, these are the runner beans that are tamed via trellises or left in the wild. A popular legume in this genus has been named the scarlet runner, owing to its surprising mix of shades of pink beans in the pod, from mauve to violet and deep scarlet to a swirl of purples. While it might very well be the biggest bean of all (and therefore could be mistaken for belonging in the *P. lunatus* genus), the creamy white bean appropriately called the Royal Corona is another type of runner. Made popular by bean champion Steve Sando, the Royal Corona is of Mesoamerican origin and measures in at nearly twice the size of a lima bean, getting even bigger while cooking.

Also in the broader Fabaceae family are some of the most loved ingredients used by cooks far and wide. Peanuts are a well-known favourite across the world, taking many forms from salted snack to boiled in the shell, and from nut butter to the famous African groundnut stew. Those familiar with the western Asian spice fenugreek find that all parts of this legume are perfect for a uniquely flavoured dish.

While not in the Fabaceae family, but with similar botanical characteristics, ground cover that sometimes acts as feed for ruminants and other animals can also be legumes. Alfalfa and clover, like most legumes, have unique root nodules that absorb nitrogen from the air. They convert this into the nitrogen they need to grow and help replenish the soil while also cleaning the air.

Vanilla beans are also not a bean but rather belong in the orchid family, despite their name. The salty, succulent Salicornia, which had fifteen minutes of fame in the mid-1990s, is another misnamed ingredient. It is not a legume, despite gaining its culinary notoriety as the sea bean.

Sowing the Seeds

From the start of their lives beans are readying themselves for the challenge of being planted again, or eaten. Most bean plants are hermaphrodites, meaning they bloom with both female and male parts. As such, they can self-pollinate and

Pole beans climbing cornstalks in a garden.

continue to regrow on their own without the help of pollen from other plants. With the seed doing double duty as the bean, they can be harvested for your eating pleasure or saved and replanted again. This self-sustaining characteristic is what has preserved the abundance of colourful heirloom varieties that can be seen at local farmers' markets today.

Growing beans depends largely on the resources available. Most like warm weather and some even have a high tolerance for extreme heat. Watering needs vary widely, depending on the bean type and the climate in which they are grown.

Choosing which beans to grow can also depend on the amount of space available. There are three basic growing methods that can be applied, depending on what the bean needs; pole beans climb and therefore need a support, runner beans typically have long tendrils and often need a trellis to tame their wild behaviour, and bush beans (not to be mistaken with the American family brand, of course) are independent and grow without the need for assistance.

For the creative gardener, choosing a proven Native American technique that yields more than just beans, such as the Three Sisters companion planting method, might prove both fun and rewarding. The 'three sisters' are corn (maize), beans and squash. When planted together, the tall stalks of the corn become a trellis for the beans, the beans provide nitrogen for the other two plants to grow and the squash leaves cast shade that keeps moisture and nutrients in the ground.

Of course, both the bean type and the method which you would like to use to grow them will require certain things from the location in which you plant them. A site that allows for plenty of sunlight during the day is optimal. Most beans need to be watered and fed regularly too, so planting in close proximity to a water source is recommended. Test the soil in

Early Native American men and women cultivating a field and planting corn or beans, 1591.

which the beans are being planted; beans grow best in soil with a pH of 6.0–6.8 and this can be adjusted if needed.[2]

Bean plants announce that they are getting close to an edible stage when beautiful flowers start to bloom. Flowers are followed by seedpods that will mature to develop beans that can be enjoyed 'green' or dried and saved for future cooking or harvests.

If the objective is to harvest dried beans, waiting until the pod is sufficiently dry is key. The bean seeds inside the pod will be firm, and this indicates that it is time for picking. Waiting until the pods are brittle will make it difficult to collect the beans, whereas if there is any moisture remaining, mould may be imminent. Grab a solid gathering bag and a friend or two, and begin pulling each pod from its branch. Choosing a strong or tightly woven tote-type bag will allow for easy separation of pod and bean; just fasten the end and smash the bag against a hard surface to separate the beans from the pods.

Sorting beans from any remaining debris.

Whole pods, not just seeds themselves, can be dried too.

Pods of green beans strung up to dry are often called 'leather britches', referring to a slang term for trousers. The method is used to preserve the beans, most commonly in the Appalachian area of the United States.

The front of Thomas Jefferson's Monticello.

The experimental gardener might take a few notes from former American president Thomas Jefferson. An avid world traveller at the turn of the eighteenth century, Jefferson often returned to his home at Monticello in Virginia to research and experiment with new-found plants and techniques. Jefferson chose beans to grace the vegetable gardens that overlooked the vineyards at Monticello, planting scarlet runner and purple hyacinth beans along the arbours.[3] The trellises were looped with deep lavender and white flowers and pods when the plants were in bloom, often getting as near as 6 metres (20 ft) tall, serving as both shade and a dramatic vineyard setting in the hot summer months.

For those who are in search of a more diverse garden, or are just curious about the flavour and texture of beans

Sweet Pea.   Hyacinth.   Sun Flower.

Published by J. THACKARA & SON ENGRAVERS 35 Spruce St. Philad.ª

James Thackara & Son Engravers, hand-coloured etching of a bouquet with a purple hyacinth, sweet pea blossoms and a sunflower, 1814–17.

Beans can be found in a variety of colours, shapes and sizes.

beyond the types that have been grown and marketed through very recent history, such as navy beans, black beans, pintos or kidney beans, a simple rule is to shop for colour or name. While not always guaranteed, finding beans (or seeds) that are colourful or have a uniquely mottled or dotted exterior is a good indicator of an heirloom varietal or something unique. A step further might also be to look online for seed-saver sites that sell unique species and order them for experimentation.

2

Bean Beginnings

Man's predecessors didn't experience cooked food for thousands of years. As with many inventions, it is speculated that our Neanderthal ancestors stumbled upon fire by accident, in a lightning (mis)fortune or in the act of pounding stone slabs for another purpose, which generated sparks. However it occurred, finding fire was a turning point for humanity in many ways. They now had command over their surroundings, and fire became a source of protection, warmth and even holy significance.

Fire was a turning point in eating too. Though it is not known exactly when or how cooking began, it is certain that fire propelled its discovery. Until this point, humans were familiar with beans in their fresh form, what we would now call a green bean, but these wild species were most likely stringy and an endless chew. In its ability to change the structure of a food, cooking allowed for such unpleasant or otherwise inedible foods to be consumed. Because heat releases proteins and carbohydrates, breaks down fibres and often increases nutritional value, an increased and diverse selection of plant and animal substances was now available for consumption. Humans now had control over what they were eating and for how long they could preserve it.[1]

But it would not be until around 4000 BCE, with the rise of the first stratified civilization of Sumer, that cooking would branch off into cuisine and beans would first suffer their social stigma. Before the creation of Sumer, from the Paleolithic to Mesolithic periods, hunter-gatherer societies generally divided labour by gender; women collected plants and men hunted and fished.[2] The harvesting of beans and other vegetation looked much like today's concept of foraging. With farming and large-scale agriculture not yet a reality, early humans would find what was available where they lived with enormous dependence on the seasons and weather conditions. Wild species of beans were some of the foods commonly found. With no existing leadership in their small communities and little wealth discrepancy (concepts that can be contrasted with food-producing, organized civilizations), the focus was solely on survival. In comparison to impending structured societies like Sumer, researchers widely agree that these prehistoric communities tended to be more harmonious.

After the Mesolithic Period came the Neolithic, and with it, the Neolithic Revolution. Also known as the Agricultural Revolution, this period of time was another turning point in the history of food. Archaeologists believed that this event occurred due to the natural warming of the environment after the Ice Age. A long period of barrenness gave way to a climate conducive to cultivating plants and farming began. This organized system of growing food was not to be mistaken for agriculture, a much larger and environmentally intensive format of producing food and fibre that would arrive later.

The trial-and-error activity of systematic plant and animal domestication began to make its way across the Old World. No longer were societies – large or small – having to lead nomadic lifestyles to find their food. Instead they were

Japanese drawing of *mame*, or bean plants, showing vines, leaves and pods, *c.* 1878.

learning to take control of their environment and make it work for them, in a wearisome and often discouraging process. It is commonly believed that grains were among the first plants to be farmed, and the first to fail. Just as the humans were acclimatizing to new places as they migrated, so were the plants and livestock that settled with them. So-called weeds became of value and were harvested as well. Rye and oats, now commonplace, were originally dismissed. Luckily for us, the tomato was rescued from fields of corn and beans.

The age of discovery was also an age of destruction. In an attempt to learn, grow and expand, this newly found cultivation was exhausting the soil. In a foreshadowing of what would come years later with the development of mass agriculture, it was not yet known that to plant so often was to deplete the soil of its nutrients, inhibiting further food growth and straining essential environmental resources. People weren't yet aware that it took only a few years to exhaust soil, but up to fifty years for it to restore itself. Land that had been overworked and overgrazed turned to desert.

During this time, quite a few familiar foods were under cultivation. Wheat and barley were first, then peas, lentils and other legumes, and later olives, figs, dates, grapes and pomegranates. Grains are often given the credit of having the starring role in the Neolithic Revolution but, as bean historian Ken Albala states, legumes played an influential part as well.

By no means a sidekick, but never given the credit as a protagonist, legumes were the first on the scene to be recognized as improving the growth of wheat and, later, vegetables. Legumes provide a natural fertilizer when planted near other crops. Their root systems fill with healthy bacteria called rhizobium, which pull nitrogen from the atmosphere, feeding and repairing the soil. Ruminants such as cows and sheep, which require a plant-based diet, can eat what humans don't, replenishing the fertilizer. Healthy soil and plants mean cleaner air for all to breathe. And in a reflection of the world in which we live, eating both grains and beans proves effective for the human diet. Sometimes containing even more protein than meat, beans work synergistically with grains in the diet to provide essential nutrition.

This realization, coupled with an administrative system to govern the newly formed canals and systems of irrigation, made the new process of food production smarter, paving the way for civilizations to develop. Fuelled by this new-found discovery, population growth surged. 'Without the beans, it is certainly less likely that these early civilizations would have ever arisen,' Albala notes.[3]

One of the most widely used legumes today for this nitrogenous resource, lentils were also among the first to be discovered. Found in the Fertile Crescent, lentils would come to support civilization. Self-pollinating and weather-tolerant, over time, the wild lentil grew to become a sturdier plant with a thinner coat which allowed for faster germination and easier digestion. As a nutritious plant suitable for small amounts of land, the lentil lent itself perfectly to domestication and, as a food source, increased the human population.

As with farming, the civilization of Sumer then also arose out of the Neolithic Revolution. In Mesopotamia, between the Tigris and Euphrates Rivers in what is now southern Iraq, Sumerians formed what is thought to be the first stratified society, just south of where lentils had more than likely first been domesticated. Unlike the relatively egalitarian groups that preceded them, the Sumerians operated on a much larger scale and formed a hierarchal structure. Many were farmers, so the scribal society documented what they grew: grains such as barley, wheat and millet, legumes like chickpeas, lentils and beans, and produce such as garlic, leeks, cucumbers and mustard were all logged in cuneiform script.

In addition to the lentil, two other legumes believed to have come from the Fertile Crescent are the fava (broad) bean and the chickpea. The fava bean is widely credited with being the first bean in existence; archaeological findings near Nazareth date as far back as 6500 BCE. Egypt embraced

Lentils ready for preparation.

Despite being one of the first beans to be discovered, chickpeas continue to have a strong presence in today's cooking.

the fava perhaps more than anywhere else. To this day it is a primary component of the Egyptian diet, with *ful medames* claiming its status as the national dish and a breakfast staple.

The chickpea, also known as the garbanzo bean and the Egyptian pea, is in fact a bean and was found to have originated near Turkey and Syria. It spread, becoming an integrated part of cultures in Greece, Italy and Spain. In Arabic, chickpeas themselves are called *hummus*, not to be confused with the popular dip made with the same ingredient, which is correctly titled *hummus bi tahini*.

But with the formation of social classes in Sumer came beans' reputation – one that remains in Western societies today. Where the wealthy were more interested in and could afford to eat meat, beans were the first staple to be eliminated from their diet, leaving them to be linked with the poor.

The end of the Ice Age had dried up bodies of water in northern parts of the earth, creating dry land where there had formerly been large seas between Asia and Alaska. Researchers believe this made it possible for migrants to travel east, crossing into what would later become North and South America, bringing their own foodways and established knowledge with them. Transfers of culture, diet patterns and new growth across the planet could now occur. Since they were easily transported, satiating and adaptable to a range of climates, beans were among the items stowed away for new homes.

3
Bean Cultures

Excavations of the Spirit Cave in Thailand have shown archaeologists the possibility that beans and peas were cultivated as early as 9750 BCE. Following that time period, from 7000 to 5000 BCE, across the planet in the Americas, wild vines of runner beans were among the plants being harvested by the inhabitants of caves in the Tamaulipas Mountains of Mexico. Though the beans were not yet domesticated, it is thought that this group of people were experimenting with the control of other plants, such as summer squash, chillies and gourds. Not too far away, in the Ancash region of Peru just north of Lima, beans were being farmed. From 2300 to 1500 BCE, the great Indus cities of Harappa and Mohenjo-Daro near present-day Pakistan, where it is speculated that the chicken first became domesticated, relied on a meal consisting of wheat, barley and field peas spiced with mustard, cooked in sesame oil and seasoned with turmeric or ginger. The Scythians of the ninth century, a nomadic people of central Asia whom Hippocrates called 'a fat and happy people', primarily relied on their cattle for nourishment, given that the stability of agriculture could not be a part of their roving routine. However, as they moved they traded, often for food for their herds. Alongside fish and other basic foodstuffs, beans were a preferred supplement. Around the sixth century, oils were in demand for a range of purposes, from cooking to lighting to medicine. Many kinds were extracted, including some from legumes: soybean and coconut palm in Asia and groundnut (the earliest form of peanut) in South America.

From Old World to New

The Romans had a particular devotion to beans, especially the fava bean. While the rich subsisted on a diet of loaves of wholegrain bread, wine and their favourite beans, the Roman poor did not experience them in the same way. They had limited access to cooking facilities so bought food when they could from street vendors. Handfuls of olives, figs and raw beans became a regular part of the diet and, if lucky, a slice of roast pork or salted fish.

But at the dawn of the Common Era, the Roman Empire began its fall and with it went their uncompromising loyalty to the legume. In 476 CE, Romulus was overthrown by the Germanic leader Odoacer, the first Barbarian to rule Rome.

Today, loyalty to favas in Italy is preserved by the ongoing tradition of using the Modica cottoia fava bean. Modica, a UNESCO World Heritage Site in southeast Sicily, until recently sustained itself economically with agriculture and livestock farming. This particular bean was used to feed cattle after having been interspersed in the cereal crop fields to add nitrogen to the soil. Its abundance meant it became established as a feature of the local cuisine too, where it earned the name 'cottoia' since it was easy to cook. As meat consumption increased, however, cultivation of this particular fava bean has seen a decline.[1]

It should be noted, however, that despite the Romans' devotion to beans, we find among them an aversion to lentils.

Frontispiece to a 1709 edition of *De re coquinaria*, supposedly written by Apicius in the 1st century CE.

In fact, their distaste for the little legume meant that it was more suitable as a castaway; an estimated 800 tonnes used as packaging filler during the shipment of the famous Vatican Obelisk. Ironically, it was in Rome that one of the first known cookbooks was written, *De re coquinaria*, supposedly by Apicius, which did contain some lentil recipes. Despite the written attempt by Apicius, perhaps a closeted fan, the predisposition against lentils was carried over into medieval Europe, where dried peas and beans were much preferred owing to their double duty as feed for animals.[2]

Though dairy products were available to Asia and the Arab worlds, milks made from pulses and nuts dominated the market, a trend that continues there to this day. With the exception of the Tang Dynasty from 618 to 907 CE, when a clotted cream called *su* was 'in', more often than not China made its milk from soybeans. Considered the 'Great Provider', the soybean was both spiritual and practical. Just as the people of India also believed, food was directly tied to the health of the body as well as the mind and soul. In the case of plant-based milks and subsequent foods such as bean curd, the advantage lay in the fact that they wouldn't sour like animal milks did, so the risk of intestinal discomfort was low.

In 1492 Columbus sailed the ocean blue. By 1493, for better or worse, he had catalysed what would become one of the most pivotal points in the homogenization of our world today: the Columbian Exchange. Having lost their way to the East Indies, he and his crew colonized an inhabited island in what would become the Bahamas and continued exploring this New World. By exchanging new plants, animals and diseases among the two different hemispheres, the natural environment as well as the economic, social and political climates of the world shifted seismically.[3] An Italian by birth, Cristoforo Colombo was an explorer hired by Queen Isabella I of Castile during the last year of Spain's oppressive *Reconquista* efforts, as a part of her imperialistic plan that would succeed in positioning Spain as the first global power.

Though more widely known today for the potato, Peru also has a connection to the bean and, unfortunately, to those who remained in Spain's *Reconquista* regime. In 1525 the Spanish conquistador Francisco Pizarro attempted to conquer Peru. He founded Ciudad de los Reyes so he could establish roots for himself and his men there, a haven where they could defend themselves against the native people as he fought for Spanish reign. The Incan people, still recovering from another recent attempt at a takeover, attacked Pizarro but were defeated. In 1535 the city was renamed Lima, after the bean native to the area and in reference to *limaq*, which means 'speaker' in the original spoken language of Quechua.

Mostly coming from the southern parts of the Americas, the items that crossed the Atlantic into the Old World form an impressive list: potatoes, tomatoes, maize, avocadoes, pineapples, chocolate, vanilla, peppers and even items like gold,

Young soybean plants.

Bowl of New World beans.

silver, rubber, chewing gum and quinine. The list includes legumes too: peanuts, butter beans, lima beans, scarlet runners, haricots and others. The Americas benefited from the food trade as well; Columbus would later bring wheat varieties, chickpeas and sugar cane to the Caribbean. Yams and cowpeas were introduced when the Old World explorers began to bring their African slaves.

Sometimes the foods that were being exchanged between both Eurasia and the New World were not readily accepted in the Old World. It was roughly three hundred years before New World products were truly embraced there. But there were three that found themselves welcomed with fairly open arms: turkey, tobacco and beans. The Old World already had many legumes, making for an easier adjustment to beans such as the lima coming to the table; chickpeas and lentils were commonplace in Europe and the kidney bean was already known as the French bean. The Chinese, already with a large population needing nourishment, embraced the peanut along with sweet potatoes – both New World items that would later become Chinese food staples and would be woven into other Asian cuisines as time progressed.

To this point, the world had operated more or less on a trade system, bartering for the needs of each community. The Columbian Exchange opened the floodgates for global economic trade markets as we know them today and began to blur the cultural lines of rituals, practices, ideas, languages, politics, recipes, flavours and traditional knowledge. A new, homogenized yet complex interplay between this New World and the Old would now form, shifting ecosystems and creating new social constructs.

Some foods that were brought over to the New World largely demonstrated the foodways of the captives that came with them and began to create cross-cultural exchanges that would forever change both agriculture and ethos in the places from which the foods had travelled. Groundnut stew is an example: while peanuts originated in South America, it was their journey back to Africa with the slave trade that would root their identity in the westernmost region. British colonists longed for the flavours of home, such as Indian curry, another cross-culture dish, and replicated it with groundnut stew. Made with groundnut paste (or peanut butter, today), palm oil, smoked fish and goat meat, the stew soon became engrained in Ghanaian culture. And with time, while the British became further detached from the story, the stew became a comfort food more closely identified with all of West Africa.

Bean-eaters

Beans were, and still are, often tied so succinctly to certain groups of people that their identities became synonymous with them. In many cases, the beans were a staple if not survival food for those who had less, having been left behind by the rich as they ate their way up the food chain. In any case, beans sometimes planted roots so deeply in a specific locale that it was nearly impossible to find a table without them.

Africa had many legumes for which they can claim roots. The cowpea, pigeon pea and hyacinth bean all originate from and were consumed across sub-Saharan Africa. Much like the Three Sisters method of the Native Americans, cowpeas were often grown alongside grain cereals, and later maize, in parts of Africa so the beans could have a natural trellis to grow up. Rice and cowpeas, served together, would become a symbol of strength during times of hardship, particularly for the people of Senegambia, who were some of the first to journey abroad as captives to the new land. Meatless at the time and known as *thiebou niebe*, this would later become the dish that was Americanized as Hoppin' John, offering prosperity at every new year. Senegambians began to influence their new community, reinforcing their own cuisines and establishing a new culture.[4]

In Mexico, we find that beans are so fully integrated that they have become a staple in every home, in nearly every dish. Though often seen together with rice by outside cultures, the beans themselves are the focus of the people of Mexico. They are roasted and eaten alone (*frijoles de la olla*), or as fillings and substance in tortillas, tacos and soups. Refritos, or refried beans, may arguably be the most well-known Mexican bean dish, having its origins in indigenous pre-Hispanic culture as a way to stretch food for as long as it would last. In sweets such as the signature pan dulce, the concha or the empanada, sweetened bean purees make for a soft and smooth filling.

The Italian love for the bean has continued throughout history and into the present day. The Tuscan diet is often centered around beans and lentils, particularly what are known as fagioli or white beans (*fagioli* is also the broader Italian word for any type of bean). Food anthropologist Carole Counihan thoroughly documents the foodways of the Florentines in her book *Around the Tuscan Table*, noting the prominence of beans in token Tuscan dishes *fagioli all'uccelletto*, *farinata*, *zuppa lombarda*, *pasta e fagioli* and versions of *minestre*. The love of beans was so apparent that the Tuscan people were even called *mangiafagioli*, or bean-eaters. A 'Hymn to the Bean', also available in snide pop culture variations, can be found expressing this devotion.[5]

> Hail to the bean
> Divinely Florentine
> To which nature gave a heart shape
> Just like the fateful human organ.
> Covered deliciously with the sweet oil of the Tuscan hills
> Baptized with generous Chianti and sweet fruit.
> Brothers of the table let us raise
> The centuries-old hymn: Hail to the bean!

Boston, one of the oldest cities in the United States, was nicknamed 'Beantown' quite by accident. In Colonial New England, where Boston sits now, beans and brown bread were a common dish. The Plymouth colonists were used to eating a rich, dark bread and the Native American baked beans with maple syrup. The English adopted the dish and its cooking method, eventually using molasses to sweeten it but keeping the traditional bean pot, for a while. But this was the early 1600s and, though the dish did become Boston baked beans in the early 1700s, it still wasn't anything that truly defined Boston culture. What put Boston on the map as Beantown was a publicity stunt aiming to promote 'Old Home Week' in 1907. Stickers, a new invention at the time, were widely released that

Homemade refried pinto beans with chips and lime.

pictured two shaking hands over the top of a bean pot that read 'Come back to Massachusetts'. An article went out in the *Boston Globe* and postcards were sent that read, 'You don't know beans until you come to Boston; Bigger, Better, Busier, Boston', with an image of a bean sprout, and 'Souvenir of Boston and Vicinity, Won't You Have Some?', with an image of a bean pot.[6] The infamous bright red candy Boston Baked Beans, made with the legume peanuts, were then produced by the Ferrara Pan Candy Company in the 1930s.

Diets and Food Trends

Beans are a powerhouse of nutrients and can be a nearly complete source of nutrition for those who need it. In places throughout the world where dietary practices consist mainly of protein and carbohydrates, beans are an affordable and accessible solution to creating a more balanced diet. Often mistaken for a starch, much like rice or pasta, beans are indeed a vegetable.

Filled with high amounts of protein, fibre, soluble fibre, complex carbohydrates and micronutrients (vitamins and minerals) such as vitamin B and calcium, beans are beneficial for everyone, and in particular those with diabetes and heart-related diseases. Beans' gradual absorption into the body helps those that need to regulate their blood sugar and the fibre is good for hypertension and other cardiac-related health.

But the concept of 'beans, beans, the magical fruit' seems to have overtaken many a person's desire to be healthy by way of eating beans for fear of the resulting association with them: flatulence. A fear of farting in public after eating legumes can be traced to Platina's *De honesta voluptate* (On Honest Indulgence and Good Health) of 1470 in which he blames lentils for flatulence and suppression of the 'amorous urge' all at once. Nearly four hundred years later, physician William Alcott (uncle of Louisa May Alcott) wrote that beans lead to flatulence, acidity and other disorders. Oddly enough, this was at the conclusion of his book promoting vegetarianism to the people, in which he previously placed beans on a pedestal and made a nutritional case for their consumption.

Those who suffer from flatulence fright are justified, at least when it comes to dried beans. These, unlike their fresh counterparts, contain indigestible compounds called oligosaccharides. This particular series of offenders demand special bacteria from your gut to swoop in and break things down for digestion in a fermentation process creating a combination of hydrogen and methane – a formula for what eventually becomes passed gas.

At least two attempts have been made to grant those who want to enjoy beans without the digestive complications access to an alternative. At the University of California, Berkeley, in the 1970s, the 'clean bean' was designed by food engineer Benito de Lumen, who genetically reconfigured the oligosaccharides so they would metabolize in the human body just as a fresh green bean would, instead of fermenting. It didn't catch on.[7] A few years later, the British researcher and owner of Peas and Beans Ltd Dr Colin Leakey set out to create a hybrid of a bean he had found in Chile a number of years prior with the goal of it being 'low flatulence'. Dr Leakey called his bean the Prim bean, saying it was more prim and proper than other beans. Though he did sell upwards of $16,000-worth of his dignified bean, he ultimately concluded that flatulence is a good and normal thing for a person to experience.

The risk-takers who recognize the value of beans and have cooked them throughout the centuries have a number of theories about how to eliminate or reduce the discomfort. If soaking, skim or discard the water completely before cooking. Doing so will remove the gases that have already started to accumulate but may also take away some of the accrued flavour and even vitamins. In the same vein, St Francis of Assisi warned that soaking beans would perpetuate unnecessary worry. If jumping straight into cooking, help yourself out by adding some Mexican epazote or a strip of Japanese kombu along with other initial seasonings, both of which have been long-theorized to relieve stomach cramping and general digestion. There are theories that regular consumption may build immunity, though this has never been proven, and, of course, taking anti-gas pills like Beano before eating might help with prevention.

Throughout history, legumes have particularly served as a meat/protein replacement in vegetarian as well as more recent vegan diets. Western monasticism has an early recording of strict vegetarianism by way of St Benedict, followed by the Carthusians, who religiously relied on beans for their nutrients.

Before Pizarro officially overtook Peru, the Incan diet was primarily vegetarian. Despite an abundance of game meats and though guinea pigs were raised in every household, the protein foundation of their diet was beans, peas and avocados, accompanied by a variety of other vegetables. Similarly, a major basis of the Indian vegetarian diet is the lentil, or dal, stemming from the ability to grow them easily since the earliest of times.

Vegetarianism became a pillar of the Nation of Islam when the faith was formalized in 1930 and, with it, beans took the form of dessert. A separatist movement that empowered black identity and taught self-reliance and independence, the Nation of Islam favoured abandoning anything representing an enslaved past. Those who followed left other religions behind, replaced surnames with an X and maintained disciplined diets. Since many ingredients and dishes of the time in black culture were also reflective of a 'slave diet', they were discouraged. Soul Food in particular was called out, not only as an obvious depiction of the horrific occurrence, but because the Nation's leaders saw the high fat and sugar content as yet another way in which white men were attempting to manipulate and control black people. As such, the diet that had been consumed by slaves, passed down as waste from the whites, was forbidden.

Elijah Muhammed took the reins of the Nation of Islam in 1934 and during that time wrote 'How to Eat to Live', guided by the Nation's dietary principles of both identity and health. He promoted their governing vegetarian diet supported by whole grains and vegetables, enforced limiting sugar and 'soul foods' like collard greens and corn, and stood by Muslim law in forbidding pork, alcohol and tobacco altogether. While most beans were also prohibited, navy beans were valued. Elijah Muhammed wrote, 'Allah (God) says that the little navy bean will make you live, just eat them . . . He said that a diet of navy beans would give us a life span of one hundred and forty years. Yet we cannot live [half] that length of time eating everything that the Christian table has set for us.'[8]

One particular dish, bean pie, became a favourite among the dishes made with the prized New World legume. Bakeries began to offer the pie made with cinnamon and nutmeg, beans whipped until they became an airy custard filling. Baked and served in a whole-wheat crust, the bean pie was simple to make and a favourite of those who embraced the new lifestyle. It rounded out meals of smoked turkey or tofu, brown rice and vegetables with a nutty and sweet dessert.

Landing on restaurant menus and becoming a staple in corner shops, the pie quickly became mainstream not just among the newest Muslims, but more broadly in African American culture. The vegetarian dessert caught on, replacing the traditional sweet potato pie. Muslim American historian Zaheer Ali likened the substitution to the replacement of one's imposed slave name; in some ways, the bonds that tied them to slavery were lifted.

In the 1960s, during the Vietnam War, long before the buzzword 'sustainability' had anyone's attention, counterculture cuisine was an integral part of the many other civil rights movements. In an act of political solidarity, the Baby Boomer generation often organized and protested; they wanted citizens to have the right to know where their food was coming from and for corporations to have accountability and demonstrate responsibility. All of this would play a part in the resurrection of the vegetarian movement while

Agricultural bean fields at Seabrook Farm in Bridgeton, New Jersey, 1942.

simultaneously paving the way for what we know it to look like today.

Since the advent of counterculture cuisine, a fixation with being healthy has been at the forefront of people's minds. Fad 'elimination' diets took a stranglehold, passed from one generation to the next, often taking on new names with just slight variations in procedures or what was approved (or not) for eating with each new turn. Beans seem to be at the top of the forbidden list each time. In 1992 the Atkins Diet was relaunched, with the book *Dr Atkins' New Diet Revolution* becoming a *New York Times* bestseller for five years straight. In 2003 the South Beach diet rivalled the Atkins Diet, both emphasizing lean meat proteins and restricting carbo-hydrates. In 2009 Whole30 launched a month-long weight loss plan based on eight suggestions for 'eating real foods', excluding grains, legumes, dairy and baked goods. In early 2013 the Paleo Diet suggested we eat more like our early ancestors, consuming more meat, nuts and vegetables. Owing to their starchy content, beans were not approved in any of these cases, some of which cited the phytates present in beans. (Phytates are natural plant defences that act as anti-oxidants and have been shown to act as enzyme inhibitors in the body. Most enzymes are proteins.) Numerous other bean-free diet plans have been sold on TV or marketed at weight-loss centres.

However, eliminating beans from the diet is nothing new. Though Pythagoras was a vegetarian all the way back in around 600 BCE, he didn't eat beans. One could theorize that this was due to some perfectly practical reasoning from this philosopher's innate wisdom. In fact (or, more correctly, what is believed is that), this simply came from some kind of otherworldly scare that just happened to occur in a bean field. Blaming beans, his devout followers didn't eat them. Nor did they vote, since different coloured beans were used to cast a choice.

Oddly, a more recently diagnosed disease related to fresh favas seems to have origins exactly where Pythagoras and his followers put down their roots in what is now southern Italy. Favism is a rare inherited disease in which sufferers, typically of Mediterranean origin, lack the enzyme glucose-6-phosphate dehydrogenase in their red blood cells. Most often affecting boys, the disease means that eating raw fava beans or breathing in the fava flower pollen causes an immediate attack on the red blood cells, leading to weakness and fatigue or even death.

Regardless of changing attitudes, nutritionally beans can stand alone as a powerhouse. But they are even more incredible when paired with rice, especially when the grain has had the least amount of polishing and is consumed in its purest form. When eaten together, they become what is called a complete protein. In addition to the good nutrition one would get from simply eating beans or grains, the two items eaten together form a yin and yang bond of protein strength. The various amino acids not present in beans are present in the grain, while the lysine (also an amino acid) that is lacking in grains is provided by beans.

In the 1980s anthropologist Dr Sidney Mintz proposed the theory that most people in the world typically eat along what he called the core-fringe-legume pattern. Mintz's pattern consisted of the core: a carbohydrate such as a potato, yam, cassava, cereal grain or product such as pasta; the fringe: an enhancement to the core – anything that helps it to taste better, from complementary animal proteins to garlic, cheese or salad greens; and the legume, whose presence Mintz observed in the routine meals of most cultures throughout the world.[9] Building on Audrey Richard's earlier studies of the Southern Bantu people, the Bemba, who typically ate a thick porridge made of millet, a relish of vegetables and accompanying meat or fish, Mintz's philosophy was to examine which of the three components most people ate more of.

Veganism, the dietary practice that takes the ethical and environmental values of vegetarianism a few steps further, made its formal debut in England in 1944. Donald Watson, an animal rights activist, formed the Vegan Society and defined the term as 'non-dairy vegetarianism' to his mere 25 subscribers. In 1951 the group broadened the loose restriction to include all animal products and added the lifestyle philosophy that vegans are those who choose to live all aspects of life without the exploitation of animals.

> One may become a vegetarian for a variety of reasons – humanitarian, health, or mere preference for such a diet; the principle is a matter of personal feeling and

Dragon's tongue beans.

varies accordingly. Veganism, however, is a principle –
that man has no right to exploit the creatures for his own
ends – and no variation occurs.[10]

At the time of Watson's death in 2005, the Vegan Society
noted an estimated 250,000 self-identifying vegans in Britain
and over 2 million in the USA.[11] But the Vegan Society wasn't
the first to declare such principles and, since then, vegans'
dietary practices have dictated new revolutions within the
food science realm, using everyone's beloved legume, the
chickpea.

Before dairy, meat and egg substitutes became mainstream, Watson's work would have been inspired by physician

Sir Kensington's Fabanaise line of products are made with a chickpea base of aquafaba.

Dr William Lambe of London and Percy Bysshe Shelley – his understudy – both of whom dedicated their diets to plant matter, authoring books such as *Water and Vegetable Diet* and dabbling with an early vegan method of eating called the Pythagorean diet. Since then, good vegan food options in a mass market of over-processed foods have been limited, often consisting of mock meats made from commodity soy product. But with the uptake of veganism continuing to rise, innovators looking to find a sustainable alternative have set their sights on a possible disruptor.

In 2014 vegans with a bent for baked goods rejoiced at the announcement of aquafaba, a quick DIY egg white alternative simply made by whipping the liquid brine of canned beans.[12] Vegan musician Joël Roessel anonymously posted the discovery on a cooking blog after noticing the liquid foaming and doing some experiments. After going public, the musician demonstrated that aquafaba could be used for making anything that called for a frothy egg white base, from meringues and whipped marshmallow fluff to French macarons and foamy cocktails like the Ramos Gin Fizz.

While most have found that chickpea brine is the most reliable in making aquafaba, experiments have continued with other bean brines, including using the flavourful 'pot liquor' remaining after cooking dried beans. Celebrity chefs and bartenders across the world have begun to use it in their kitchens and bars, both as a creative ingredient and as an added offering to vegan guests. It has found a home as the base in the carefully crafted mayonnaise alternative from the Sir Kensington's condiment brand and, in early 2018, inspired 535 people to crowdfund more than $25,000 in just forty days in order to produce the dairy-free butter substitute Fababutter.

4

The Lore and Literature of Beans

With beans so indelibly linked to the development of cultures throughout history, it should come as no surprise that they play a role in the way that these cultures express themselves. Beans make central appearances in the stories passed down, the rituals performed, the songs sung and the art left behind by one generation after another.

Some of the earliest thinkers actively rejected beans. If Pythagoras wasn't already making a somewhat unreasonable case for not eating beans because of his bean field fright, he added to his philosophy that flatulence quite frankly conflicted with a clear mind. Aristotle agreed, adding that the hollowness of beans' roots was more than likely a ladder to the gates of Hades. For this reason, he also avoided bean fields and added that a partially consumed bean left out in the sun to rot would smell of the semen or blood of someone who has been murdered.

Despite Aristotle being technically wrong, in that beans do not have hollow roots but extensive nodules, there is some rationality in philosophizing that beans mirror our souls' generation and transitions. The root words for bean in Greek and Germanic languages indicate 'a swelling out'. As bean historian Ken Albala points out, this could refer to bloating in connection with flatulence, as Pythagoras is saying, but also to the bean pod that grows much like a woman's stomach when she is pregnant. As a result, the bean became connected with regeneration and fertility.[1]

As one can see, folklore and fables serve as potent sources of socialization, passing along cultural norms disguised as easy-to-follow slices of entertainment. The well-worn fables of Aesop have survived many generations to remain a prominent part of modern culture. Children today continue to get perhaps their first exposure to the classist notion that beans are a staple of an unsophisticated cuisine through the tale of the Town Mouse and the Country Mouse. Town Mouse pays a visit to his country cousin and, after turning up his nose at Country Mouse's meal of bacon and beans, drags his simple friend into town for a proper meal. When the pair barely survive the perils of fine dining with their hides intact, Country Mouse departs, leaving his exasperated kin with the story's moral, 'Better bacon and beans in peace than cakes and ale in fear.' Danish author Hans Christian Andersen spun another legume-related tale that has managed to survive and find its way into childhoods around the world for nearly two centuries. In the Princess and the Pea, a single pea is hidden beneath a stack of mattresses to stress the importance of sensitivity towards even the smallest of things. Perhaps the most famous piece of bean folklore offers little in the way of moral nourishment. In the English fairy tale Jack and the Beanstalk, a series of morally dubious decisions leads the young protagonist to acquire a set of magical beans and begin a fantastical journey up both the beanstalk and the socio-economic ladder.[2]

In addition to lore, beans have also made their way into the folk traditions of various cultures. For centuries now, in a ritual known as *mamemaki*, the Japanese have sought to

A cartoon depiction of a Japanese woman throwing beans to soldiers for good luck, 1904–5.

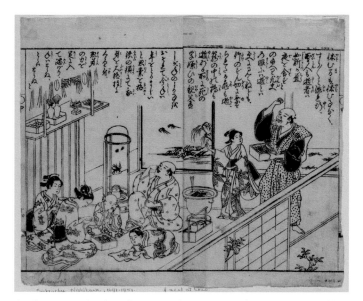

Setsubun mamemaki, where family members are eating beans accompanied by a man about to toss a handful of beans into the room, 18th-century print.

cleanse themselves of evil spirits by throwing beans during the Setsubun celebrations held each year on the day prior to the start of spring. Throughout the world, but particularly in Sicily, Catholics carry dried fava beans to celebrate St Joseph's Day and demonstrate gratitude for the hearty crop that helped them to survive a catastrophic drought. In a similar bid for sustained prosperity through beans, one tradition of the American South holds that serving black-eyed peas on New Year's Day will bring about good luck for the coming year.

Not just preserved in historical traditions, beans continue to find a place in the popular culture of recent generations. They insert themselves into modern-day aphorisms. In Boston someone who is ignorant 'doesn't know beans'. To let a secret slip is to 'spill the beans'. To be 'full of beans' might mean that a person is either highly energetic or downright

Black-eyed peas are the bean used in Hoppin' John.

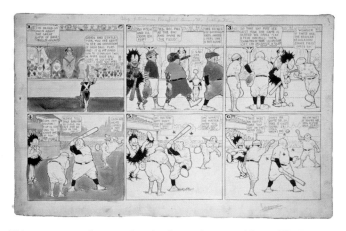

This 1913 watercolour comic strip shows characters Nemo, Flip, Impy and Doc playing baseball for the Lilliputians. Doc is 'beaned' and a fight breaks out.

nonsensical. Accountants and bureaucrats can be dismissed as mere 'bean counters'. If you throw something and hit someone you've 'beaned' them, and if that something is a baseball it can be said that you threw a 'bean ball'. For a moment 'cool beans' served as a fashionable way to express approval.

And yes, beans are indeed a magical 'fruit' and could very well stand to be eaten at most meals. But what triggers this childish rhyme, making we, even as adults, begin to recite it at the mere mention of what is simply a source of sustenance? The schoolyard chant that appears to have its origins in Britain has made its way around most of Western civilization, making a name for itself in classic cartoons, sketch comedies, sitcoms and even Stephen King novels, with at least thirteen known variations, including one dedicated solely to favas.

Beans even cement their place alongside the stars of the silver screen. In a memorable scene from *Casablanca* (1942), American film legend Humphrey Bogart as Rick Blaine

Annibale Carracci, *The Beaneater*, 1580–90, oil on canvas.

concedes that in the grand scheme of things the troubles of his cohort 'don't add up to a hill of beans in this crazy world', while in *The Silence of the Lambs* (1991) Sir Anthony Hopkins brings to life Thomas Harris's most haunting literary creation, Dr Hannibal Lecter, who chillingly proclaims that he has consumed one of his victim's organs in a dish thoughtfully paired with fava beans and wine.

Beans have made many appearances in recent popular music. Dean Martin romanticized 'pasta fazool', an Anglicization of the classic Italian dish *pasta e fagioli*, in his timeless number 'That's Amore'. British rock pioneers The Who not only included the jingle 'Heinz Baked Beans' on their album *The Who Sell Out*, but the record's front cover featured an image of lead singer Roger Daltrey holding an oversized can of the product while bathing in beans. For the film version of *Tommy*, Ann-Margret took Daltrey's place, writhing around in the beans that spewed forth from her broken television, among other advertised products. Country music legend Johnny Cash borrowed the age-old have beans/have-not trope for his song 'Beans for Breakfast', while grunge rock royalty Nirvana relegated their playful little tune 'Beans' to the rarities bin. Even The Beatles couldn't escape the bean. The Fab Four had to take to the airwaves to request a reprieve after they were lovingly pelted with jelly beans by adoring audience members at some of their early U.S. shows.

In twentieth-century American literature, beans reaffirmed their identity as sustenance for the destitute. They appear regularly in the works of John Steinbeck, whose characters, frequently travellers in search of survival if not prosperity, consume the humble bean to keep their bellies full. In his novel *Tortilla Flat* (1935), Steinbeck addressed their significance directly, 'Beans are a roof over your stomach. Beans are a warm cloak against economic cold.' A few decades later, as the Beat Generation embraced the nomadic, ascetic lifestyle, they also embraced the same simple culinary staple. The wanderers in Jack Kerouac's *On the Road* (1957) and *Dharma Bums* (1958) consume cans of pork and beans to survive along their journeys, ascribing a sense of romance to the simple meal.

Not much to look at apparently, the bean never established itself as a dominant feature of the visual arts. However, certain notable artworks and artists have included it in their images. Italian painter Annibale Carracci produced a pair of studies of *The Beaneater* in the late sixteenth century, depicting a man raising a spoonful of beans, most likely the Tuscan fagioli, to his mouth. The man's floppy straw hat and meagre dress give the viewer the impression that they're bearing witness to a peasant's supper. American painter Andy Warhol immortalized three bean and two pea varieties among a wide selection of flavours for his series of *Campbell's Soup Cans*.

Cloud Gate as seen in Chicago's Millennium Park.

Spanish Surrealist Salvador Dalí sprinkled some beans beneath a grotesque image of a body tearing itself asunder in his 1936 painting *Soft Construction with Boiled Beans (Premonition of Civil War)*. Though properly titled *Cloud Gate*, a twenty-first-century metallic sculpture installed in Chicago's Millennium Park by the British artist Anish Kapoor has become known colloquially as 'the Bean' for its uncanny resemblance to a gigantic, reflective legume. The same artist installed a vertical version of the exhibit in Houston in 2018, igniting an online fury between the two cities over who wore it best, complete with legume-themed name-calling such as 'has bean'.

Some places have developed such a close association with beans that they have seeped into their entertainment and self-expression. Boston, Beantown itself, had one of its earliest baseball teams play with the moniker Beaneaters for a number of years around the turn of the twentieth century. The label didn't stick, however, as the team would sub-sequently change its name and location a number of times before eventually landing in Atlanta. New Orleans, Louisiana, is home to both a proud culinary tradition and an equally proud musical tradition, and the two frequently intertwine. Red beans and rice hold a particularly notable place in both realms. Piano giant Professor Longhair released an upbeat version of Muddy Waters's ode to the dish with 'Red Beans'. Legendary trumpeter Louis Armstrong felt such an affinity for the pair that he used to sign off letters with 'Red beans & ricely yours'. Contemporary New Orleans trumpet icon Kermit Ruffins takes the association a step further, actually cooking the dish for guests at his weekly shows. A local group, the Red Beans Parade, has even started Bean Madness. A charitable competition running parallel to the college basketball championship tournament each March, the event is held to determine the city's best red beans and rice producer. Restaurants are placed into brackets and compete against one another at public events in rounds titled the 'Sweet 6-Bean' and the 'Final Fork' until a champion is crowned.

Red kidney beans served over rice.

Jelly beans are believed to be the 19th-century mash-up of Jordan Almonds and Turkish Delight.

Beans hold such a familiar place in modern-day lives that they have donated their moniker to a variety of non-legume items around the house. Children amuse themselves watching the minute hops and gyrations of 'Mexican Jumping Beans', or *frijoles saltarines*, a real but unrelated botanical seed inhabited by a tiny larva. Tiny beads used for packing volume into household products have become associated with beans: bean bags serve as an informal and inexpensive replacement for chairs and sofas; and Beanie Babies, stuffed animals filled with tiny beads, loom large in popular culture after having had their moment as one of the most widespread product crazes of the past few decades. And of course, not just for 'beaning' The Beatles, the jelly bean is a gelatinous, sugar-laden, bean-shaped sweet that has cemented its place among American candy staples. Commonly found in nondescript flavour and colour combinations, gourmet brands such as Jelly Belly have made an art form of crafting jelly beans in a wide variety of exotic or even intentionally disgusting flavours.

5
Bean Cuisines

Without culture, we wouldn't have cooking. Without cooking, we wouldn't have cuisine. From the cooking of a pot of beans that often has so many perpetually perplexed to fried fritters and sprouted seedlings, beans have proven themselves culinarily versatile.

Originally found in Incan archaeological sites, the nuña bean can be 'popped' into a food still eaten in areas of Ecuador and Peru today. The seed can be found in more than thirty varieties, running the colour spectrum from bright red to yellow and speckled. When fried in a shallow pan of oil, it will burst, exposing its inside and transforming into an airy afternoon snack. The result looks similar to popcorn and tastes like roasted peanuts.

Two Brazilian bean-based dishes have strong ties to Africa. *Feijoada*, Brazil's national dish, was traditionally made as an inky rich and spiced stew of black beans and low-on-the-hog cuts of meat like pigs' ears, trotters and tails, and beef tongue. After having been brought to Brazil by Portuguese colonizers in the sixteenth century, African slaves conceptualized the comforting dish for their masters. Considered a celebration dish even then, it is now commonly made with salty, smoked pork or beef cuts and is served on the weekend

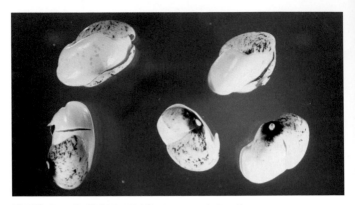

Nuña beans after being popped.

or during times of occasion with rice, farofa (toasted manioc meal) and batida (a Brazilian spirit similar to rum mixed with lemon juice and sugar).[1]

Acaraje is a small bean patty with a big story. Served as a snack on the streets of Bahia in Brazil, it is a mixture of mashed black-eyed peas, ground dried shrimp and onions. After being fried, they are sliced in two and stuffed with onions, okra, shrimp and pastes made from nuts. The falafel-like fritter has its origins in Nigeria, where it is called *akara*, meaning 'ball of fire' in the Yoruba language, owing to the chilli paste it is served with and fiery orange colour that results from the *dendê*, or palm oil, that it is fried in. But fierce flavour isn't the only reason *acaraje* is so special. The technique of making it has become significant to those that practise the Candomble religion, the Afro-Brazilian tradition that originated with the slave trade in the early nineteenth century. With connections to Africa lost through systemic racism, the ritual of food preparation was a way to preserve identity. In particular, the recipe and skill for making *acareje* – *akara* – was passed down. As a result, the craft of making *acaraje* is officially protected by the Brazilian government in honour of its cultural heritage.

Soy sauce has made it so far into the mainstream that most people no longer even question its origins, but it can be found in history referenced as early as 160 BCE, on record from the Han Dynasty. Traditional recipes include a mash of soybeans and wheat that is drained and then allowed to ferment over an extended season. When it has finished fermenting, any fungus that has developed is removed and the resulting 'cake' is covered with salt brine. Now at the brewing stage, the remaining liquid after weeks in brine is soy sauce, a richly flavourful substance that can naturally add a balanced but intense taste that develops into an umami flavour in many dishes. Historically strained before bottling, in more recent times the liquid is also pasteurized.

Other variations on soy sauce include ageing after bottling or regionally specific methods of preparation. In Japan, for example, where soy sauce is called *shoyu*, the use of different cultures (*koji* in Japanese) is common in making soy sauces. Also common is a higher ratio of wheat to soybean in each recipe. In Indonesia, soy sauce is known as *kecap*, a catch-all

Feijoada, Brazil's national dish.

A man grinds beans on the streets of Seoul, Korea, *c.* 1901.

word similar to condiments and also the cognate for the word 'ketchup'. *Kecap manis* is the most commonly used variety of Indonesian soy sauce. A much thicker, sweeter version than the original Chinese recipe, it is employed during cooking as well as used as a dip in traditional and street-food dishes.

Similarly, soybeans are an integral part of the fermentation methods long practised in India. The indigenous and tribal nations of this area of the world have been fermenting a variety of vegetables and plants for more than 2,500 years, the results becoming a fundamental part of their diet. Today, fermented products made from soybean seeds or pastes can be found particularly in the eastern Himalayan regions of

Nepal, India and Bhutan. A source of income for those in the rural areas of Manipur, *hawaijar* is a sticky, fermented soybean paste consumed in a variety of ways. *Chagempomba* is a special occasion dish for the people of Manipur, made with *hawaijar*, rice and vegetables. *Kinema* is another example. A recipe based on whole soybeans, this fermented dish is an income generator for the women of the eastern Himalayas and is eaten in the style of curry and with rice.

Most commonly used in confections, the adzuki is another bean found frequently throughout Asian food cultures. Introduced to Japan from China around a thousand years ago, it

Sampling beans on the street in Chemulpo, Korea, *c.* 1903.

became a staple of both cultures' cuisines, as well as other areas conducive to growing varieties of the bean, such as Korea, India, Taiwan, Thailand and the Philippines. Though its delicate flavour is also appreciated, it is the deep red colour that it carries over into cooked products that is particularly prized, especially when making sweets for holidays such as Chinese New Year. Most often, adzuki beans are made into a sweet paste, called *ahn*, that is used to fill cakes and confections. In other cases, they are soaked and made into milk like the soybean, popped like nuñas or roasted and served as a coffee substitute.

Closely related to the adzuki are mung beans. Believed to have originally grown in India over 4,000 years ago, mung beans are also known as *moong dal* or simply *moong* in the Hindi language. Used most often in its young sprout form, the bean itself can be found in colours of yellow, brown, black or green, depending on the variety, and it is used in both sweet and savoury dishes. In the USA they were also of interest to farmers in the mid-1800s, where they were known

An ornately designed traditional mooncake.

Purchasing bean cakes from a peddler, *c.* 1890.

as chikasaw peas. Their popularity is now predominant in Southeast Asia, primarily in China, Thailand, Japan, Korea and Vietnam, though ongoing consumer interest in South Africa has led to (relatively unsuccessful) experiments in growing them commercially there for the last few decades. Mung beans are often prized for their starchiness and are the base for the transparent noodles found in many Asian cuisines. In large developed markets today, mung beans often appear as glassy bean sprouts in the produce section of Asian grocery stores.

Like the adzuki, when ground into a paste the mung bean is used as a filling in the traditional Chinese mooncake celebrating the Mid-Autumn Festival. Dating to the Song Dynasty of the eleventh to thirteenth centuries, gifts would be offered to the moon each autumn. In China and Taiwan specifically, mooncakes filled with bean or lotus seed pastes became a preferred gift of choice. Elaborately decorated on the exterior, the cakes are most often made with a lard-based pastry and typically have salt-cured duck eggs hidden inside for added symbolic blessing. The traditional gifting has translated into today's culture as a present from businessmen to their clients and between families. Mooncakes are said to possibly have been the inspiration for the Japanese fortune cookie owing to the surprise treasure that is found inside.

Many varieties of bean find their place at the breakfast table in quite a few countries around the world. In both Pakistan and Israel, chickpeas are favoured for their creamy texture. Pakistani people use them at breakfast for *halva poori*, a dish made of spicy chana masala, a sweet tahini confection and unleavened fried bread, while a traditional breakfast from Israel may contain shakshuka (eggs baked in tomato sauce) and a side of pita and hummus. A typical Mexican breakfast wouldn't be complete without *refritos* or soupy black beans, and a Venezuelan breakfast makes use of their own customary fried dough pockets, *arepas*, filled with beans and white cheese, for a substantive start to the day.

One country's bean-based breakfast has origins as early as the 1300s and is still going strong today. The full English breakfast was founded by the Anglo-Saxon gentry who, though not royalty themselves, were considered to be a priv- ileged social class. Their bountiful breakfast table became a hospitable gesture for incoming friends and family passing through the country and the recipes and quality of ingredients a status symbol. Until then, breakfast had been fairly absent from the tables of the masses, who relied on lunch and dinner for their meals. With exceptions made for children, the sick, the elderly and working men, breakfast was considered glut- tony by the Catholic Church, who viewed it as an act of eating too much too soon.

But it was the gentry's desire to both posture and be hospitable that would disrupt the meal's service for years to

The iconic Heinz Beanz can is still sold with its captivating blue label today.

come. The full English breakfast caught on and was further refined during the Industrial Revolution in the late eighteenth century. The Victorians then brought their eye for elegance and exotic tastes to the table. Though they studied the breakfast ways of the gentry, they added their own flavour, upgrading the extravagance from presentation to ingredients used, in unmistakable Victorian fashion.

While the gentry had set the table, and the Victorians had perfected it, it was during the Edwardian era that breakfast became standard and accessible. Also known as the golden age, in this era breakfast became synonymous with garden parties and leisure. Since it had become commonplace for everyone, not just royalty or upper classes, to have breakfast at the start of their day, gathering spaces such as hotels and other meeting places made accommodations to begin serving the first meal as well.

Full English breakfast.

The widespread demand for a sensible, energy-packed start to the day that could also be easily mass prepared began to redefine the foods that were served in a full English breakfast. In 1903, ketchup company Heinz launched the British favourite HP Brown Sauce, an item that would soon become a condiment staple for the most diehard full English breakfast fans. In doing so, Heinz securely established brand recognition in the United Kingdom and, in the 1960s, was able to capture housewives with their blue-label canned baked beans for breakfast too.

The full English breakfast was an affordable, hearty meal that served the rising workforce and also began to take on differing identities throughout the country. Also known as a 'fry up' today, a full English breakfast might consist of back bacon, eggs, sausages, baked beans, a fried tomato, fried mushrooms, black pudding and fried and toasted bread, though it would really depend on where you are and who is cooking. From the north to the south of England, the authenticity of black pudding's placement within a fry up is often debated. In visiting Scotland, one might find that a full Scottish breakfast also contains haggis or, in Ireland, white pudding in lieu of black and some Irish soda bread instead of toast, or the addition of some Irish potato cake.

The Modern Culinary Bean

Today, the world is inundated with options. Information is limitless and provided to us at nearly every turn, solicited or not. Technology and data transfer have shaped the way we have cooked for centuries and continue to do so with recipes, cooking advice and even grocery shopping available at the touch of a button.

We can see this transition begin to happen in Mexican food. Because of the Columbian Exchange, Mexican cuisine went from bean cuisine to beef cuisine. With the arrival of the Spanish *vaqueros*, the Americas now had cowboys, cattle and new cooking techniques. The practice of grilling meats and adding a 'side' of cowboy beans began to catch on. The native South Americans went from a diet relatively low in fat and high in vegetables and legumes to one that was heavy in meat and dairy products. Tortillas, originally a maize recipe, were now being made with wheat, and chili, a dish made with beans and tomatoes, transformed into chili con carne.

Up until this period, the Mesoamerican people primarily in the Yucatán area of Mexico used the farming system *milpa*, a practice of intercropping fields of corn, beans and squash during a set amount of time followed by a fallow period to

Cowboy beans are now often called chilli beans and have regional variations.

restore the soil. Colourful varieties of beans could be found, each offering their own nutritional value: mustard-yellow Amarillo bola, rosy bayo, cream mantequilla, periwinkle or purple ayocote, maroon-mauve pinto and mottled red and white vaquita rojo.[2] The tiny tepary bean grew in many colours and was prized for its high tolerance to drought. Known to have been cultivated as far back as 5000 BCE in the arid lands of central America, the *t'pawi* ('it's a bean') became a culinary staple particularly for the Tohono O'odham tribes of the Sonoran region of what is now the state of Arizona.[3]

But America soon became a melting pot of cuisines from around the world as migrants settled and introduced their

ADAMS'
PATENT
BEAN AND SEED SEPARATOR.

Hundreds of bushels of refuse beans are taken to market annually, such as blighted or split beans, dirt and gravel stones, and the same freight paid on such as the best beans. They condemn the good beans and not near their value is realized.

We offer to those who raise and deal in produce, ADAMS' PATENT SEPARATOR, which will thoroughly cleanse beans from all dirt, bring out the split beans by themselves and separate the medium from the pea beans as well as the marrowfats; thus increasing the market value some 25 or 30 cents on the bushel, while the refuse saved at home is valuable for sheep and fowls.

Different grades of meshes are substituted that will separate oats from barley, wheat and buckwheat, and take out all foul seeds. They can be fitted to all Fan Mills. Also open meshes that will sort and take the sprouts off from potatoes.

The above Machines will be seen in operation at STEVENS, BROTHER & CO. 222 Pearl St., N.Y., R. L. ALLEN, 189 & 191 Water St. or at the Manufactory, No. 5 Batterman Block, Lincoln St., Boston. Orders solicited and promptly attended to.

SANFORD ADAMS,
Inventor and Proprietor.

REFERENCES.

Sanford Adams advertises its Bean and Seed Separator, marketing it as also useful for grains and potatoes.

Placing cans of pork and beans in shipping crates, 1915–25.

foodways. Beans were a staple component of many dishes that are still sometimes made today in the eastern part of the United States, such as cowpoke beans and bean hole beans.

Until the early nineteenth century, beans had only been eaten from fresh pods or cooked from dried; canned navy beans and frozen green beans hadn't yet come about. The American Civil War began in 1861 and feeding troops across thousands of miles became complicated. Though railways, riverboats and other methods of transport could deliver them dry goods, a procedure for keeping military forces at optimum health with perishables like fresh fruits, vegetables and milk became crucial. The Commissary Department approached Gail Borden, a teacher, real estate agent and general jack of all trades, who was experimenting with canning milk, commissioning him to provide non-perishables for the northern army. It proved a success, and soldiers returned home after the war with an acquired taste for consuming food this way. By the late 1800s, nearly thirty million cans containing a variety of foods were publicly available across the nation.[4]

With the efficiency and quantity of production, canned goods were economical too. But fraudulent companies began to cheat consumers, cutting the amount of a product or knowingly filling cans with contaminated food. Since the food inside wasn't visible and cans weren't branded, consumers didn't know what they were getting until it was too late. The Campbell's Soup Company saw an opportunity and began to create labels with illustrated ingredients. They even offered a branded campaign with their Campbell's Kids, who were visibly healthy, vibrant and smiling. Unheard of in the early twentieth century, this game-changing marketing move influenced the Minnesota Valley Canning Company to put a positive spin on a product they thought would never sell due to its irregularly large size: a new variety of pea called Prince of Wales. The 'Green Giant Great Big Tender Peas' soon had their own identity with a true-to-form mascot named the Jolly Green Giant. Large and friendly, the human-like figure appeared on the label holding a big and seemingly heavy green pod full of plump peas.

Cans of food would be of further and greater use in the Second World War, providing sustenance exclusively to the troops, since metal was one of the many items that were rationed. After the war, in a dismal economy, canned foods

Jolly Green Giant statue resurrected in 1979 on Route 169 in Blue Earth, Minnesota.

offered affordable and filling meals to the recovering masses. But by the beginning of the 1950s, another new technology began to shape how people were eating and how beans would be sold. In 1952 the television set could be found in twenty million homes across America. At around the same time, an executive of C. A. Swanson & Sons, a company in the business of buying and selling frozen poultry, met with Frozen Dinners, Inc., a company in the business of making in-flight food for Pan Am's international flights. He saw their three-compartment tray and, in 1953, the first 'TV dinner' was released to the nation. It featured turkey, gravy, stuffing, whipped sweet potatoes and green peas with butter, and was sold at 98 cents per tray. Modern and on-the-go families took the hint and shifted from the dinner table to the television set, enjoying their heat-and-eat meals and newfound entertainment. The frozen food industry only grew from there, shifting from full dinners to sides such as macaroni cheese or frozen carrots, single items like burritos, and steam-and-serve snacks such as edamame.

Derby Chili Con Carne advertisement, 1940s.

Even with the rapidly changing food culture, beans have nearly always been available as a dried good, stored and ready to be cooked at the chef's convenience. In the 1970s Rival Manufacturing purchased and rebranded what we now know as the crock-pot or slow cooker. Debuting it at Chicago's National Housewares Show, they marketed it as an appliance that took 'as much electricity to run as an incandescent light bulb' to housewives looking to prepare a hearty meal easily.

But the crock-pot hadn't always been about full meals. When Irving Naxon got a job as an engineer at Western Electric, he started tinkering with inventions of his own. Naxon was inspired by *cholent*, a slow-simmered dish of meat, potatoes and beans traditionally eaten on Shabbat. Knowing his grandmother had previously used a crock-pot to cook her *cholent* overnight in the residual heat of an oven, Naxon placed a patent on his 'Boston Beanery' in 1940 and marketed it as a bean cooker that could slowly simmer dry beans until they were fully cooked. By the late 1970s the number of crock-pots sold was in the millions.[5]

In the 1980s sales slumped, but in 2013 Consumer Reports noted that 83 per cent of American households had a slow cooker. While Rival Manufacturing's promise was that the pot 'cooks all day while the cook's away', based on the idea that dinner would be slow-cooked and ready at the end of a typical work shift, in 2012 the makers of Instant Pot rolled out their line of programmable pressure cookers aimed at 'anyone looking to save time in the kitchen while providing nutritious, well-balanced meals'.[6]

During the Boston Beanery's advent, it was quick-cook meals that housewives were looking to prepare, so crock-pots, canned goods and time-saving recipes were gold. In 1955 Dorcas Reilly worked at Campbell's kitchen, which tested recipes for placement in low-cost pamphlets that the soup company could easily get into housewives' hands. Reilly saw an opportunity to use the so-called 'Lutheran binder' (a mushroom soup), already widely used as a casserole filler in Midwest dishes, mixing it with the widely popular frozen green beans. But the grey colour of the soup had to be hidden; Reilly topped it with crispy onions and the company marketed the Green Bean Casserole as a holiday dish due to its festive colours.

Two women stringing beans, c. 1930.

Crock-pot sales may have sunk in the 1980s because more people were dining out than ever before. A flood of new restaurants had appeared on the American scene, with nearly every urban corner offering multiple varieties of cuisine to tantalize taste buds and suit budgets of any type. In a nearly parallel timeline to the development of the technological advancements made for eating at home, the culinary industry experienced a creative new wave and expansion too.

This growth was a completely new experience for generations who had grown up on a 'beanery'. The term Naxon had used in his patent for the crock-pot had formerly been the affectionate expression for a cheap place to grab a hearty eat and often tepid beer. Traced to the mid-1800s, a beanery was a lunch room that prided itself on affordable, filling food that was aimed at the working class. A full bowl of pork and beans (from which the slang name was derived) might cost six to nine cents and meals were served 24 hours a day, all week long.

Though pork and beans became the staple menu item and, later, the iconic dish of beaneries, they weren't the only foods that the early, diner-like restaurants offered. Corned beef, roast beef, chicken pot pie and even other meals such as the typical American breakfast of ham and eggs filled the menus. Guests looking for a full meal could fill up on 30-cent combinations that might include sides of bread, a slice of pie and hot coffee.

In 1920 John 'Barney' Anthony created what would later become a chain of beaneries in California. Barney's Beanery first opened in Berkeley, but for a male clientele only. After operating as a solo businessman, doing everything from cooking the food to scrubbing the floors, Anthony decided to move the beanery to West Hollywood on Santa Monica Boulevard, at the time a fairly desolate part of the Historic

Route 66 situated adjacent to more agricultural fields than skyscrapers. Anthony's decision paid off, making him famous among celebrities and well known for his generosity in giving away food.

Those who used the space as their own escape included Clara Bow and Jean Harlow and, in the 1940s, Clark Gable and Bette Davis graced the tables. Newshounds that covered Hollywood happenings often reported actors, musicians and comedians having a presence at Barney's, chattering among themselves about which celebs might be giving Anthony their spicy news. Not too long after that, the casual restaurant underwent some cosmetic changes: rooms were added and televisions installed.

In 1964, just four years before his death, Anthony posed for an article in *Life* entitled 'Homosexuality in America', positioning him in front of a controversial sign that prominently hung from the top shelf of his bar that read, in all capital letters, 'Fagots, stay out'. The image's caption offered a quote from Anthony himself, defiantly saying 'I don't like 'em.'

But the public stance didn't ruin Anthony's own public persona, at least among celebrities. Artist Edward Kienholz had been pondering a Beanery replica since 1958, but took advantage of the newfound attention and, in 1965, created the interactive 'The Beanery' in the restaurant's parking lot. The 8-metre (22-ft) long walk-in from Keinholz was made from plaster of paris and papier-mâché figures with clock faces that read 10:10 a.m. and smelled of sizzling bacon. The avant-garde artist had been inspired by a newspaper headline that read 'Children Kill Children in Vietnam Riots', and suggested that the horological faces resembled eyebrows, but more so that the Beanery's patrons were wasting precious time. In the artwork, Anthony was the only person depicted without a clock for a face.

Those that knew Anthony, including his loyal celebrity friends, also vouched for him. Actor David Barry told the *Los Angeles Times* in 1977 that 'no one had ever paid much attention' to the sign, and 'Barney's always had a regular gay clientele.'[7] Eventually it was thought that the local police had ordered the sign, having had a history of homophobic discrimination. However it went up, activists wanted it down and, in the 1970s, a coalition of gay rights activists rallied to successfully pull it from the bar. The sign now sits in the ONE National Gay & Lesbian Archives at the University of Southern California Libraries.

Though Anthony died on 25 November 1968, celebrities have continued to find solace in the space he created. The Doors saw the story of the sign as a message to check out the rebellious Beanery, and everyone from Bette Midler to Bob Dylan to Drew Carey frequented it. The second Barney's Beanery followed soon after Anthony's passing, increasing to a total of six locations to date, including a massive mixed-use expansion of the original West Hollywood location that was announced in 2018.

Although not as infamous, Boston Beanery: Restaurant and Tavern also continues to use the term and serves modern American fare, with three locations in the eastern part of the U.S. as of 2018. As beaneries evolved and time progressed, hamburgers, hot dogs, sandwiches and speciality items like milkshakes and even pizzas have been added to appeal to consumer tastes, adopting the menu of the American-style diner many are familiar with today.

6

The Bean of Tomorrow

On 17 April 2013 in the dry plains of West Texas, a fiery explosion sent a mushroom cloud into the air at a fertilizer plant, killing the workers inside and even some residents in the town nearby. The fertilizer plant processed and stored ammonium nitrate, a highly combustible and somewhat volatile chemical, and a preferred fertilizer in industrial farming. Developed in 1909 by Fritz Haber and Carl Bosch, synthetic nitrogen was originally used to power U.S. and European weapons during the Second World War. After the war was over, a surplus of this newfound form of nitrogen remained and the U.S. government had the perfect audience to sell it to. Knowing that farmers needed nitrogen to grow food, they promoted it as a yield-boosting, labour-saving option. For a world in recovery, this also meant an injection of cash for farmers and food for the people. But with it, legumes were widely displaced from the agricultural equation as the relied-upon natural nitrogen source. The world's food supply now had a chemical dependency.[1]

For a while the miracle growth of these chemical soil-saviours worked, allowing farmers to increase production and expand their businesses. This also meant they could make large-scale equipment purchases, such as tractors and

Migratory bean pickers are provided transportation to the bean fields via school buses in Delaware, 1940.

combines. More and more farmers went into the business of growing only one or two crops, finding that a shift away from field rotation and planting a diverse array of options meant a faster and more lucrative return. Most began to grow 'commodity crops' that could provide the ultimate gain – corn, wheat, cotton and soybeans that could be sold on the international market to Europe and Asia. But sadly, the good times wouldn't last for most family farmers and the abundant food that was now produced needed a place to go. Whereas farming had previously been a practical source of food and income for families, industrial agriculture had now taken root as the food source for our world. The added quandary of what to do with the resultant excess food led to the pervasive, highly processed forms we see today that are marketed with catchy words and labelled with unfamiliar terms.

The production of beans took a turn too, taking on a very different appearance as a large-scale crop than what one might have seen previously or even now in a back garden. As with other mass agriculture, the number of varieties being grown dwindled down to three or four of the easiest-growing and quickest-selling types.[2] Since the science of growing beans can be a guessing game from bean to bean and season to season (and therefore a matter of income versus loss), agriculturalists generally choose one type and make it their speciality.

When thousands of rows are grown over a large acreage, hand-harvesting is out of the question. At just the right time, a tractor rolls by, cutting each plant and leaving the pods to dry on their branches on the ground for a while longer before they are collected. When it is determined that they are dry enough for separation, another machine comes by with a conveyor belt attachment, shaking the pods over a screen that allows the beans to fall through, further sifting any debris.

The New Soybean

Of all the crops that suffered from the Second World War, corn and soybeans probably took the biggest beating. They were both ancient seeds and diet staples, and standing in a fully grown field of either prior to the war could have meant an unrivalled experience of picking a super-sweet snack straight from the stalk. Added value products, items made from any initial food source, remained relatively unmodified up to this point.

Soy sauce became a good example of an added value product that transitioned from the highly traditional to the massively produced. Unless soy sauce is labelled naturally or traditionally brewed, most of what is found widely in groceries today is what is known as chemically hydrolysed liquid seasoning, which is made by treating soybeans with hydrochloric acid, neutralizing the resulting liquid, adding caramel colouring, salt and corn syrup, and finishing with preservatives. Compared to the traditional method, this soy sauce is not as rich or balanced in flavour, but rather a one-note salty substitute.

The twenty-first century saw the introduction of Soylent and the Impossible Burger, both soybean-based foods that have employed the use of new advances in food technology. The first, Soylent, is a meal substitute formula made with a base of soy protein isolate. Named for the soy lentil food described in the 1966 science fiction novel *Make Room! Make Room!* by Harry Harrison, the original plain Soylent drink debuted in 2014. It is made by producer Rosa Foods and sold on the premise that 'food wastes more than just our time'; Rosa also states that the meal replacement has all the essentials of a balanced diet. Since its launch, the product line has added flavours to its line-up, including a coffee flavour/caffeine mix, along with food bars in 2017. The food bars have since been discontinued.

Impossible Foods promises the improbable with their plant-based faux-meat Impossible Burger that 'delivers all the flavor, aroma and beefiness of meat from cows'.[3] Made with

Large-scale agricultural fields focusing on limited varieties of crops.

Endless commodity soybean fields in America's Midwest.

soy leghemoglobin, the meat alternative is able to produce heme, which gives the product a distinctive blood-like colour and taste. In 2017 the *New York Times* published an article stating that the United States Food and Drug Administration (FDA) was concerned that the soy-based ingredient had never been consumed by humans but, in July 2018, Impossible Foods announced official FDA approval. Other ingredients that make up the burger include water, textured wheat protein, coconut oil, potato protein and natural flavours. The product is being increasingly sold in restaurants throughout the USA and Hong Kong and, in 2019, Impossible Foods announced a partnership with fast food giant Burger King to offer Americans a meatless version of their signature sandwich The Whopper.

Today, a freshly picked soybean isn't something a person would enjoy eating straight from the agricultural fields. With its move from craft to commodity, the soybean takes on a very different identity now, and politics are no exception.

Just before his first midterm elections, in 2018, American president Donald Trump received notice from European Commission president Jean-Claude Juncker that American-grown soybean imports would increase significantly if Trump agreed to end threats of punitive tariffs on the German car industry. Junker felt the push after Trump ignited an international trade war, causing multinational unrest. Since the European climate isn't suitable for growing soybeans but does heavily rely on the inexpensive crop for animal feed and milk production, the u.s. has found considerable value in this agreement over the last years, exporting 37 per cent of its soybean production in 2018 – a growth from just 9 per cent the previous year. The soybean strategy became concrete evidence that the bean has fully transitioned from humble legume to competitive currency.

Genetic Modification

In the late 1970s a herbicide chemical company named Monsanto began to study biotechnology crops. Ten years later, the company shifted gear and began to hone their experiments specifically within the area of transgenic crops, expressly the transfer of genes from other species with regard to corn, cotton, soybeans and rapeseed (canola). In 1996 Monsanto released their first transgenic product, soybeans that had been genetically modified to withstand being sprayed by Monsanto's signature herbicide Roundup. Other Roundup Ready products soon followed and were sold on the mainstream market.[4]

However, Monsanto can't take credit for genetic modification. In 1856, in the greenhouse gardens of a Moravian abbey, a monk named Gregor Mendel began to experiment

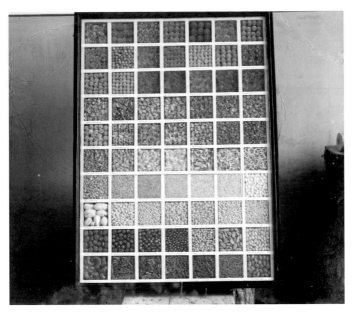

Display case containing dried bean and other seed specimens, *c.* 1905–15.

with new methods of science. 'Mendel's laws of heredity' would become more widely known in the early 1900s, after his death, and 'Mendel's traits' would later be called 'genes', his discoveries becoming the basis for genetically modified foods and the human genome project. Mendel's test subjects had been the popular legume peas.

In 2015 the International Service for the Acquisition of Agri-Biotech Applications celebrated the official first twenty years of commercialization of biotech/GM crops. They reported that 2 billion hectares (nearly 5 billion acres) of biotech crops – equivalent to twice the total land mass of the United States – were cultivated in up to 28 countries across the globe at that time.[5] Three years later, Germany's pharmaceutical company Bayer was forced to shed roughly $9 billion in assets in an effort to acquire American-based Monsanto.

The $66 billion acquisition consolidated competition between the two companies, particularly in the areas of seed sales and crop protection products. Selling its canola, soybean and vegetable seed businesses as well as its herbicide asset, Bayer's divestment was recorded as the largest anti-trust sell-off in American history.

The International Year of the Pulse

The United Nations declared 2016 the International Year of the Pulse, highlighting the dry form of the bean and noting its significant influence on farming and contribution to a healthy diet. Food Tank, the international think tank centred around food, picked up the campaign and promoted it all year long. Interviewing global leaders, Food Tank demonstrated how pulses can help us tackle issues arising from a wide variety of circumstances, from obesity and food insecurity to environmental footprint and water conservation. 'Just 43 gallons of water can produce one pound of pulses, compared with 216 gallons for soybeans and 368 gallons for peanuts,' founder Danielle Nierenberg noted early in the campaign. 'The water efficiency of pulses allows the plants to enrich the soil where they grow and reduce the need for chemical fertilizers.' To launch the year-long celebration, 'Little Beans, Big Opportunities' was held as a forum to discuss how pulses can meet today's global health challenges. The campaign brought together international organizations to discover how pulses could support small farmers and improve food security across the globe.

The Next Big Thing

Beans have gained momentum among food enthusiasts of all types, becoming a bridge between restaurant foodies and environmental activists alike. Steve Sando of California's Rancho Gordo has made a lifelong profession of obsessing over the colourful seed, dubbing himself the Don Quixote of beans and even launching a 'Bean Club' complete with subscriptions. As both a grower and a buyer specializing in rare varieties, his never-ending quest to unearth heirloom New World beans takes him to far-flung corners of Mexico in support of both seed-saving and farmer sovereignty. Chef Dan Barber of the famed New York restaurant and non-profit working farm Blue Hill at Stone Barns has made a name for

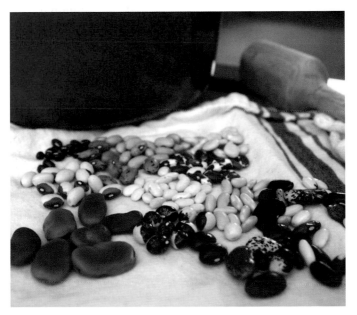

Old and New World bean varieties prepared for a pounding with the *machacadora*, a manual bean masher native to Mexico.

himself by celebrating the uncelebrated. His holistic view of how the food system works has meant a more integrated and traditional method of planting (and eating), implementing legumes for their natural nitrogenous and nutritious properties. Gary Nabhan, renowned author and ethnobotanist, based his career on the bean and thinks that they represent so much more than meets the eye. As a student at the University of Arizona, Nabhan discovered native tepary beans growing in the wild. He later founded the seed conservation organization Native Seeds/SEARCH and wrote extensively about teparies and other beans as food solutions to hotter climates. Paul Gepts, a plant sciences professor at the University of California, Davis, takes a technical approach. He and his students breed beans to be useful for growers practising organic farming. Slow Food International officially launched their Slow Beans initiative at the 2014 Terra Madre/Salone del Gusto conferences in Torino, Italy, to celebrate beans' impacts on earth and on people. At the event biennial, in 2018, beans had a strong presence in the workshops in the Slow Meat pavilion. In 2017 *The Atlantic* proposed that beans – in lieu of beef – might be the answer to the American Psychological Association's 2011 diagnosis of 'eco-anxiety'.

From farmers to professors, the team rallying behind the bean movement may have differing approaches. Some may even have opposing vantage points. But all believe that beans are essential to feeding the world.

The Future of the Bean

As we look around, the story of the little bean hasn't been so small. Its influence spans from the beginning of agriculture to the largest of fields. It has been integrated into almost

Pole beans finding their way up a broomstick.

Making tofu in the traditional way.

every food culture across the globe, providing sustained nourishment and so deeply engraining itself that rituals and songs about it have arisen, and been passed down to future generations. Throughout history, the unpretentious bean has remained down to earth. In doing so, it has interwoven its story alongside that of humanity itself.

The impact of its most valuable assets is evidenced in human nutrition and reflected in the health of the eco-system, so much so that famed Italian novelist and philosopher Umberto Eco wrote that beans 'saved civilization' once before. 'When in the 10th century, the cultivation of beans began to spread, it had a profound effect on Europe. Working people were able to eat more protein; as a result, they became more robust, lived longer, created more children, and repopulated a continent.'[6]

As we approach feeding a world of 9 billion people, one in which humans are ever more conscious of their personal health regimen and, increasingly, one in which we under-stand how that connects to an earth that needs sustaining, a return to eating and planting more beans is a well-rounded, environmentally supportive, culturally appropriate econom-ical solution.

Recipes

Historical Recipes

Lentils and Cow-parsnips
Apicius: De re coquinaria (c. AD 850)

Put the lentils in a clean saucepan. In the mortar crush pepper, cumin, coriander seed, mint, rue and flea-bane, moistened with vinegar, add honey and broth and reduced must, vinegar to taste and put this in a sauce pan. The cooked cow-parnsips crush, heat, when thoroughly cooked, tie, add green oil and serve in an appropriate dish.

Lentils and Chestnuts
Apicius: De re coquinaria (c. AD 850)

Take a new saucepan, place therein the chestnuts carefully cleaned add water and a little soda and place on the fire to be cooked. This done, crush in the mortar pepper, cumin, coriander seed, mint, rue, laser root and flea-bane moistened with vinegar, honey and broth; add vinegar to taste and pour this over the cooked chestnuts, add oil and allow to boil. When done crush it in the mortar. Taste to see if something is missing and if so, put it in, and at last add green oil.

Cook the lentils, skim them, add leeks, green coriander; crush coriander seed, flea-bane, laser root, mint seed and rue seed moistened with vinegar; add honey, broth, vinegar, reduced must to taste, then oil, stirring until it is done, bind with roux, add green oil, sprinkle with pepper and serve.

For to Make Gronden Benes

from Master Cooks of King Richard II, *The Forme of Cury: A Roll of Ancient English Cookery* (1390)

Take benes and dry hem in a nost or in an Ovene and hulle hem wele and wyndewe out þe hulk and wayshe hem clene an do hem to seeþ in gode broth and ete hem with Bacon.

Hoppin' John

from Sarah Rutledge, *The Carolina Housewife* (1847)

One pint of bacon, one pint of red peas, one pint of rice. First put on the peas, and when half boiled, add the bacon. When the peas are well-boiled, throw in the rice, which must first be washed and gravelled. When the rice has been boiling half an hour, take the pot off the fire and put it on coals to steam, as in boiling rice alone. Put a quart of water on the peas at first, and if it boils away too much, add a little more hot water. Season with salt and pepper, and, if liked, a sprig of green mint. In serving up, put the rice and peas first in the dish, and the bacon on the top.

Modern Recipes

A Simple Pot of Beans
contributed by Minerva Orduño Rincón, chef and food writer

It is the very simplicity of cooking beans which makes it so difficult. Eating a perfectly cooked bean should feel like finally sitting on that 'look don't touch' priceless antique velvet armchair in your grandmother's living room; luxuriously smooth, yielding and with just enough firmness to hold its oval shape. A perfectly cooked bean should never have a crunch of any kind – save the al dente for risotto and cook your beans until just about to burst at the seams. Beans really are exactly like a plush velvet armchair.

Soaking beans before cooking is completely optional in most cases. Unsoaked beans will take longer to cook and will need more liquid, but may in fact benefit in flavour over soaked beans, which can begin to sprout and ferment within hours of soaking. If curiosity strikes as to just how quickly a bean can sprout, place a pinto bean on a wet cotton ball on a sunny windowsill. By the next day a small green leaf can be seen poking its way out.

White tepary bean may be the exception to the 'soaking is unnecessary' rule. Even after soaking and cooking, some of these seeds will refuse to soften. The easiest way to separate these uncooperative beans is to give them a soak in warm water for an hour in room temperature, after which they will easily stand out from their plumped-up counterparts.

There are a few other crucial points to understand before cooking the perfect bean. The thick liquid holding the beans at the end of cooking is just as important, full of flavour and nutrients as the bean itself. If the goal is to make a puree of any kind, this liquid, used still warm, is the key to that smoother than silk texture. And if this liquid is so important, it deserves care. Skim the thick cappuccino foam off the pot with care and skim it often. To prevent foamy spills, use a much larger pot than you feel you need.

Perfect beans need a steady cooking tempo. They taste their best when, after boiled briefly, they're allowed to cook at a strong enough simmer to allow for movement within the pot. The beans should swoop from one place to another, not lie heavy at the bottom of the pot, which results in mushy shapeless beans.

Adding other flavours to beans is another matter of timing. A ham bone can be added from the very beginning of course, but small herbs such as thyme and Mexican oregano should wait until the foam has been removed, so as they are not lost in the cleaning process. Avoid adding acid of any kind, or salt, until the beans have begun to soften. Salt added from the beginning will not ruin the pot, but there will be a detectable crunch in the skin of the bean.

In the end, the only way to truly know how to cook the perfect bean is to do it. And eat them often.

1 cup (225 g) dry beans
water as needed

Rinse the beans well under running water. Remove any unsightly beans and debris. Place in a medium stock pot and add enough cold water to cover by about 3 inches (8 cm). Bring the beans to a boil and cook for approximately 10 minutes. Reduce to a medium simmer and cover the pot loosely.

Be sure to skim any foam from the pot during the cooking process as this will cloud the liquid. After the foam is removed, add any aromatics, sauteed vegetables, etc., as desired to pot. Once the beans have lost their bite, acidic foods such as tomatoes and salt can be added.

Cook the beans until they are almost ready to burst. The last few minutes of cooking can go quickly. It is best to note the size and fragrance of the bean rather than use a timer.

Cool the beans in their cooking liquid. Beans keep well for about five days refrigerated but freeze wonderfully. For best flavour, always store them in their liquid.

Anasazi beans *de la olla* with Mesquite Cornbread

contributed by Jeff Smedstad, chef-owner of Elote Café,
Sedona, Arizona, and author of *The Elote Café Cookbook*
and *The Eloté Café Notebook*

Beans that carbon-dated to some 1,500 years ago were discovered in a sealed clay pot in Anasazi ruins in the 1950s, and, miraculously, they sprouted. So we now have in modern times a delicious heirloom. Archaeologists based the word 'Anasazi' on a Navajo term to refer to the ancestral pueblo people of the Southwest who flourished between 200 BCE and around 1500 CE.

Mesquite Cornbread

½ cup (110 g) supersweet dried corn powder
½ cup (110 g) medium grind cornmeal
6 tbsp flour + 2 tbsp mesquite flour
½ cup (110 g) potato starch
2 tsp baking powder
1 tbsp sugar
1 tsp salt
3 eggs
2 cups (450 ml) buttermilk
4 tbsp melted and unsalted butter plus more butter
for preparing the pans

Mix the dry ingredients in one bowl and the wet ingredients (except the butter) in another. Mix the two together by hand, gently, just until combined (don't overwork the batter). Set aside to rest for 1 to 3 hours so that the cornmeal can hydrate and soften. Butter the baking dish well. I use a cast-iron biscuit mould to make individual cakes. An 8-inch (20-cm) cast iron skillet works as well. Preheat your pan in the oven or on the hob until the butter sizzles a little (don't burn it). Then add the batter. This helps to ensure a brown crust. Bake at 400°F (200°C) for 25 minutes.

Anasazi beans *de la olla*

8 cups (2 l) water
2 cups (450 g) dried Anasazi beans
1½ tsp salt
¾ tsp ground cumin
¾ tsp each ground guajillo, chipotle, pasilla and ancho chillies
1 tsp Hatch red chilli powder
6 chiles de arbol, broken into pieces
½ tsp granulated garlic
½ cup (125 g) chopped onion
1½ tsp dried oregano
½ cup (110 ml) corn oil

Combine all the ingredients for the beans in a large pot and simmer over low heat for 2 to 3 hours, or until beans are tender. Add additional water if needed. Serve hot over a piece of mesquite cornbread.

Hummus bi tahini
contributed by Sharon Salomon, MS, RDN and nationally publicized food writer

3½ cups (750 g) canned or cooked chickpeas
⅓ cup (50 ml) tahini, or more to taste
1 garlic clove, or more to taste
½ cup (110 ml) fresh lemon juice, or more to taste
1¾ tsp cumin
extra virgin olive oil
salt to taste
pinch cayenne pepper
paprika and fresh minced parsley for garnish optional

Prepare the chickpeas first. If using canned, drain and rinse the chickpeas. Pour them in small quantities onto a clean dish towel. Fold the towel over and roll them around gently until the skins fall off. Then, plunge them in water so the skins will rise to the top and separate from the beans. Discard the skins. Peeling the chickpeas is optional, but a necessary step for perfectly creamy hummus.

Place chickpeas, tahini paste, garlic, lemon juice, salt, cumin and cayenne pepper into a food processor. Process the mixture while adding 1–2 tbsp of olive oil until all is blended or it has reached desired thickness. Taste and add more salt, lemon juice or garlic as preferred.

Garnish with a few whole chickpeas, olive oil, paprika and parsley and serve.

Pasta e fagioli
contributed by Claudio Urciouli, chef-owner of Pa'La, Phoenix, Arizona

This is a version of a recipe that I have eaten since I was a kid, which was made with beans from the village of my mother near Campania in Italy. As an adult, I make it with Controne beans, oregano and chilli from dear friend and Slow Food Presidio producer Michele Ferrante. Unlike pasta and bean dishes typical of Italian meals, this dish can be eaten as a stand-alone meal. Controne beans can be found on the Slow Food Ark of Taste.

14 oz. (400 g) pasta mista, or short tube pasta like occhi di lupo
or broken spaghetti
7 oz. (200 g) Controne beans
2 cloves garlic
1–2 stalks celery
2 tbsp extra virgin olive oil
controne chilli powder and oregano to taste
extra virgin olive oil to taste

Cook the beans, without soaking first, in three times the amount of water. If you have one, a terracotta pot over an open flame is best. Add a bit of garlic and celery to the cooking water for added flavour. When they are tender but still firm, puree or mash roughly a quarter of the beans directly in the pot to keep the moisture. Next, stir in the dry pasta in two or three turns, allowing it to

absorb the remaining liquid of the beans (think of this process as you would a risotto). When all the pasta has been stirred in, add the oregano and chilli to taste. Season with salt only as needed. Ladle into a bowl and finish with a swirl of good olive oil.
Serves 4

Pasta e fagioli fritta
contributed by Claudio Urciouli, chef-owner of Pa'La,
Phoenix, Arizona

Italians are some of the most efficient at maximizing their dishes, especially when both food and money must be stretched. This dish uses the leftovers from the previous recipe and makes a great breakfast, sandwich or snack. Simply heat a pan, brushing with a thin coat of olive oil. Spread the remaining *Pasta e fagioli* in an even layer across the pan and allow it to form a crust along the bottom and edges. Allow to cool slightly and eat right away or store for later. Slice and eat as you would a frittata or sandwich between two pieces of good bread with rocket (arugula) and tomato.

Katjang/Indonesian Peanut Sauce

Before she passed away, my Oma was an amazing cook. She was Indonesian by birth and had emigrated to the Netherlands in her young adult years, picking up their cuisine and teaching them hers. Years later, she came to America where she played a significant part in influencing my own foodways and, consequently, my life's work. *Katjang* was on everything I ate as a kid, even plain steamed vegetables like broccoli, and I'm fairly sure my taste buds were wired so early due to its flavours that now it is the reason I work in food. This recipe is the one she adapted to the American products she could find.

1 cup (225 ml) water
1 cube beef bouillon

¾–1 cup (225 g) peanut butter, creamy or crunchy depending
on preference
crispy onions, to taste
sambal, to taste

Boil water with bouillon. Lower heat and whisk in peanut butter.
Add onions and sambal. Serve with steamed vegetables, over gado
gado salad, over rice, as a dip, etc.

Rajma Chawal/Red Beans and Rice (north) and *Moong Dhaal Payasam*/Mung Bean Porridge (south)
contributed by Sasha Raj, chef-owner of 24 Carrots,
a vegan restaurant based in Tempe, Arizona

India is tremendously vast – in land, language and cuisine. While
I was born and raised a solid Brahmin-Tamilian-South Indian,
quite a few of my culinary favourites are from north India. Caught
in the middle, I couldn't decide between my south Indian heart
and my north Indian tongue. So, here are two recipes that bring
everything together.

Rajma Chawal/Red Beans and Rice (north)

This is a humble dish that seems to have found its place in nearly
every cuisine in some shape or form. It's a simple, one-pot dish,
that just gets better with each day of leftovers and so this was my
staple all through college. In fact, I would drive to my best friend's
house anytime her mother would make this under the pretext of
a study session, but really to invite myself to dinner.

First, soak 2 cups (250 g) of red kidney beans overnight in
enough water to cover, plus about 2 inches (5 cm) above. Next,
once soaked, pressure cook 2 cups (450 g) rajma in 6 cups (1.75 l)
of water. This works exceptionally well in the Instapot (manual
high, 30 mins, release pressure).

To the pressure cooker with the beans add:
2 tsp jeera/cumin
1 cup (250 g) chopped onion
¼ cup (60 g) cilantro (coriander), chopped
2 tbsp ginger/garlic paste
1 tomato, chopped
1 tsp coriander powder/dhania
½ tsp red chilli powder (optional)
3 tsp garam masala powder
3 tsp Rajma masala Powder*
1 tsp salt, more to taste
juice of 1 lemon
1 tsp sugar
and enough water to cover and pressure cook for another 20
mins (Instapot – manual high, 20 mins)

Once this bit is done, it's ready. Enjoy over a steaming bowl of rice.
Both myself and my college self wish you happy eating!

*Rajma masala can usually be bought at any Indian grocery store,
but if you like to go the extra distance with spices, as I do, you can
make your own by toasting and grinding the following.

1 tbsp kasuri methi/dry fenugreek leaves
2 tbsp coriander seeds
2 tbsp cumin seeds
1 tsp cardamom seed
4–5 dried red chilies
4 bay leaves
½ tsp cloves
1 tsp mace
¼ tsp grated nutmeg
1 tbsp dried pomegranate seeds/anardana

Then, add 2 tablespoons ginger powder and 2 tablespoons dried
mango powder/amchoor. This will keep in your fridge for months
in an airtight container and is definitely worth the effort!

Moong Dhaal Payasam/Mung Bean Porridge (south)

This recipe is one that means the world to me because it is my mother's. She and my grandmother make this on occasion to celebrate a festival or religious holiday. When I was younger, my tastes were so distracted by western cakes and chocolates that I didn't fully appreciate how delicate, nourishing and nurturing this beautifully simple dish is, but luckily for me that didn't stop my mother from making it and now I relish it whenever she does. (Note: anyone who is not my mother is at an immediate disadvantage making this recipe as her only unit of measure seems to be her hand. I've done my best to translate 'this much' to cups.)

1 cup (225 g) shelled moog dhal
1½–2 cups (450 g) raw palm sugar/jaggery/vellum
4–5 cups (1–1.25 l) coconut milk
½ tsp salt
½ tsp ground cardamom
pinch saffron
coconut oil
¼ cup (60 g) cashews
¼ cup (60 g) raisins

Wash moong dhal in water until it runs clear. Boil in 2 cups (450 ml) water (additional water may be needed) until soft, then add jaggery/vellum/raw palm sugar, simmer and stir until the jaggery is fully melted. Gently mash the cooked mung beans until they are fluffy, creamy and smooth. Remove from the stove and set aside.

Separately boil coconut milk, and then cool slightly. Add this to the mashed mung beans and jaggery. If you don't wait for the milk to cool before doing this it can curdle the jaggery. Add additional coconut milk if needed to make thinner ('not too thin, not too thick – it should be like a drink, not a paste'). Now add a pinch of saffron, ½ tsp of salt and ½ tsp of ground cardamom.

Roast ¼ cup (60 g) cashews and raisins in 2 tablespoons of ghee or coconut oil and add to the top. This should be creamy, smooth and perfectly comforting whenever you're in the mood for a big bowl of 'mom-hug'.

Red Beans and Rice

contributed by Justin Beckett, chef-owner of Southern Rail Restaurant and Beckett's Table, Phoenix, Arizona

This is my version of the quintessential southern American dish, served at our Southern Rail Restaurant in central Phoenix.

1 cup (225 g) chopped bacon
1 large yellow onion, chopped
4 links andouille sausage, diced small
1 cup (225 g) all purpose flour
2 cloves garlic sliced
2 fresh bay leaves
2 ribs celery diced
1 green bell pepper, diced small
1 cup (225 ml) whiskey
3 quarts (3 l) pork broth or stock
3 cups (700 g) red beans
2 large smoked pork hocks
2 cups (450 g) andouille sausage, sliced in half moons
½ cup (100 g) Crystals hot sauce

In a large stock pot, on medium flame, sauté your bacon and onions until golden brown and caramelized.

Add the small diced andouille and continue to cook for about 15 minutes. Add the flour and stir until it emulsifies into the fat from the bacon and sausage. Continue to cook (stirring often) on a medium-low flame until the flour turns golden brown. Add the garlic, bay leaves, celery and bell peppers. Continue to cook for another 5 minutes.

Deglaze with whiskey to help lift off the flour that sticks to the pan. Add the pork broth, beans and pork hocks to the pot. Simmer until the beans are tender (approximately 80–90 minutes).

Add in the sliced andouille sausage and hot sauce. Season with salt and pepper and taste. Remove from heat and cool. Let sit overnight for best flavour or serve immediately.

Serve with a large scoop of rice and more Crystals hot sauce.

Serves 8

Tepary Bean Pie

contributed by Casey Hopkins, Director of Culinary Operations at
Cartel Coffee Lab in Tempe, Arizona

Make sure that your tepary beans are fully cooked, cooled and drained prior to starting this recipe. These beans are drought tolerant and very dense, which means they take several hours to cook. The result is definitely worth the cook time!

For crust, I tend to go with something sweeter for this pie. A pate sucree pairs nicely with this rich filling, as does a cornmeal tart dough. I prefer Thomas Keller's Pate Sucree recipe or Joy the Baker's Cornmeal Crust when I'm preparing this at home.

When I make this, I usually serve it with a Cranberry Whipped Cream and Candied Corn Nuts. When I brought this recipe over for Natalie to try, we sampled it with Hibiscus blood orange curd! Anything creamy or bright and citrusy compliments the creamy, spicy filling very well, as does a dose of crunch. Practically any nut would pair well with this lightly toasted, candied or prepared into a brittle.

1¼ cup (230 g) tepary beans
1¼ cup (300 g) evaporated milk
1 cup + 3 tbsp (265 g) granulated sugar
5 tbsp unsalted butter
1 tbsp + 2½ tsp all purpose (plain) flour
1¼ tsp ground cinnamon
½ tsp + ⅛ tsp ground nutmeg
¾ tsp ground ginger
½ tsp ground cardamom
¼ tsp ground black pepper

¼ tsp kosher salt
zest from 1 large orange
4 large eggs
1 tbsp + 1 tsp vanilla bean paste

Preheat oven to 350°F (180°C).

Melt butter on the stove just until liquid, then remove from the heat and allow to cool for no less than 10 minutes.

Use a microplane to zest the navel orange. Feel free to use a second orange if the zest does not yield much.

Measure out the sugar and combine the sugar with the orange zest. Toss the sugar with the zest until the sugar is tinted orange and the zest has been evenly dispersed.

Combine all of the remaining ingredients in the same large metal bowl, then use an immersion blender to bring all ingredients together (a food processor would also work for this). Run the blender on high for 2 to 4 minutes until all ingredients look homogenized. It is normal for the beans to not be fully pureed – some chunks and bits of skin will remain in the batter. That will not affect the texture of the pie. Leave the filling to rest and marinate for at least an hour in the refrigerator before baking. If you are preparing a pie shell from scratch, this provides the perfect window of time to roll and parbake.

After an hour, give the filling a good stir with a whisk and pour into the parbaked pie crust (it is okay if the crust is still warm, but it will likely shorten your bake time by a few minutes). Make sure that there is about ¼ inch (½ cm) of room between the top of the filling and the edge of the crust. Bake at 350°F (180°C) for anywhere from 50 to 60 minutes, until the filling is puffed and set. Be sure to rotate midway through baking and begin checking at 45 minutes.

References

1 Bean Botany

1 The Leguminosae family is so large that it is now further classified into four distinct families: Caesalpiniaceae, Fabaceae, Mimosacae, Papilionaceae.
2 Steve Sando, *The Rancho Gordo Heirloom Bean Grower's Guide: Steve Sando's 50 Favorite Varieties* (Portland, OR, 2011).
3 Today, Monticello is a UNESCO World Heritage Site, museum, research institute and non-profit organization which may be toured by the public. See www.monticello. org, accessed 16 June 2018.

2 Bean Beginnings

1 Linda Civitello, *Cuisine and Culture: A History of Food and People* (Hoboken, NJ, 2011).
2 Carol R. Ember and Melvin Ember, 'Violence in the Ethnographic Record: Results of Cross-cultural Research on War and Aggression', in *Troubled Times: Violence and Warfare in the Past*, ed. Debra L. Martin and David W. Frayer (London, 1997), pp. 1–20.
3 Ken Albala, *Beans: A Global History* (New York, 2007).

3 Bean Cultures

1 The Slow Food Foundation for Biodiversity recently added the Modica cottoia fava bean to their list of endangered foods to help reintroduce the seed. See www.fondazioneslowfood.com, accessed 15 June 2018.

2 Joseph Dommers Vehling, *A Bibliography, Critical Review and Translation of the Ancient Book known as Apicius de re coquinaria [Apicius: Cookery and Dining in Imperial Rome]* (Chicago, IL, 1936).

3 Alfred W. Crosby, *The Columbian Exchange: Biological and Cultural Consequences of 1492* (Santa Barbara, CA, 2003).

4 This snippet of information comes from culinary historian Michael Twitty's piece in *Rice and Beans: A Unique Dish in a Hundred Places*. Much more can be found on this topic in his research on the web. See https://afroculinaria.com. Richard Wilk and Livia Barbosa, *Rice and Beans* (New York, 2012).

5 'L'Inno al Fagiolo' is translated here by food anthropologist and author of *Around the Tuscan Table*, Carole Counihan. Carole M. Counihan, *Around the Tuscan Table: Food, Family, and Gender in Twentieth-century Florence* (New York, 2004).

6 'Bean Town Origin', www.celebrateboston.com, accessed 27 February 2018.

7 Jim Dawson, *Who Cut the Cheese? A Cultural History of the Fart* (Berkeley, CA, 1999).

8 Rossi Anastopoulo, 'The Radical Pie That Fueled a Nation', www.tastecooking.com, 13 November 2018.

9 Sidney W. Mintz and Daniela Schlettwein-Gsell, 'Food Patterns in Agrarian Societies: The "Core-Fringe-Legume Hypothesis" A Dialogue', *Gastronomica: The Journal of Critical Food Studies*, 1/3 (2001), pp. 40–52.

10 Leslie Cross, 'Veganism Defined', *The Vegetarian World Forum*, 1/5 (1951), pp. 6–7.

11 See www.vegansociety.com, accessed 16 June 2018.

12 America's Test Kitchen offers some tips for making your own aquafaba. See 'What is Aquafaba', www.americastestkitchen.com, accessed 26 December 2018.

4 The Lore and Literature of Beans

1 Ken Albala, *Beans: A Global History* (New York, 2007).
2 Charles W. Eliot, *The Harvard Classics Folk-lore and Fables* (New York, 1909).

5 Bean Cuisines

1 'Feijoada: "A Short History of an Edible Institution"', https://web.archive.org, accessed 13 November 2018.
2 'Fagioli nativi di Tepetlixpa' (Tepetlixpa Native Beans), www.fondazioneslowfood.com, accessed 15 June 2018.
3 Many of the beans native to the new world can still be found today through preservation efforts of organizations such as Native Seeds/SEARCH and Rancho Gordo; all are classified into the genus Phaseolus of the Fabaceae family.
4 Andrew F. Smith, *Eating History* (New York, 2009).
5 Izabela Rutkowski, 'Crock Pot Slow Cookers Are a Must for Fast-paced Lives', 6 September 2013, www.consumerreports.org.
6 'A Look at the Company Behind the Revolutionary Cooking Appliance', https://instapot.com, accessed 24 March 2018.
7 Domenic Priore, 'The History of Barney's Beanery', https://barneysbeanery.com, accessed 26 December 2018.

6 The Bean of Tomorrow

1 Geoffrey J. Leigh, *The World's Greatest Fix: A History of Nitrogen and Agriculture* (Oxford, 2004).
2 Tom Philpott, 'A Brief History of Our Deadly Addiction to Nitrogen Fertilizer', 19 April 2013, www.motherjones.com.
3 See https://impossiblefoods.com, accessed 16 June 2018.

4 Monsanto was originally founded in 1901, producing and selling the sugar substitute saccharine. See 'Monsanto History', https://monsanto.com, accessed 16 June 2018.

5 The ISAAA released a booklet giving the top ten facts about biotech and GM crops to celebrate. See Clement Dionglay, 'Beyond Promises: Top Ten Facts About Biotech/GM Crops in Their First 20 Years, 1996 to 2015', ed. Rhodora R. Aldemita, www.isaaa.org, June 2016.

6 Umberto Eco, 'Best Invention: How the Bean Saved Civilization', www.nytimes.com, accessed 18 February 2019.

Select Bibliography

Albala, Ken, *Beans: A History* (New York, 2017)

Amundsen, Lucie B., *Locally Laid: How We Built a Plucky, Industry-changing Egg Farm from Scratch* (New York, 2016)

Barber, Dan, *The Third Plate: Field Notes on the Future of Food* (New York, 2014)

De Mori, Lori, and Jason Lowe, *Beaneaters and Bread Soup: Portraits and Recipes from Tuscany* (London, 2007)

Hamblin, James, 'If Everyone Ate Beans Instead of Beef', www.theatlantic.com, 2 August 2017

Miklas, Phil, Bean Improvement Cooperative, http://bic.css. msu.edu, 28 August 2016

Mintz, Sidney W., and Chee Beng Tan, 'Bean-curd Consumption in Hong Kong', *Ethnology*, XL/2 (2001), pp. 113–28

Ruhlman, Michael, *Grocery: The Buying and Selling of Food i n America* (New York, 2017)

Wei, Clarissa, 'How a Grain and Legume Farmer Harvests Nutrition from the Soil', https://civileats.com, 1 January 2019

Winham, Donna, Densie Webb and Amy Barr, 'Beans and Good Health', *Nutrition Today*, XLIII/5 (2008), pp. 201–9

Withee, John E., *Growing and Cooking Beans* (Dublin, 1980)

Acknowledgements

My sincerest gratitude goes to my husband Chris, without whose encouragement and enthusiasm for learning I may not have begun or perhaps completed this adventure. His editing skills and, surprisingly, knowledge of beans in literature, were invaluable.

I owe a special thank you to those who contributed recipes to this project; when I first embarked on it I knew the people I worked with every day in my food community would be the ones to turn to for some of the best recipes and they showed up for me. Thank you to Minerva, for helping me to teach people how to cook a proper bean. To Chef Smedstad for appreciating the bean as much as I do, perhaps even more, and enough to lend me a recipe from his own kitchen. With thanks to Sharon, who let me adapt her 'we just do it all by feel' *hummus bi tahini* recipe for this book. A very heartfelt thank you to Claudio for his *pasta e fagioli* recipe, who said in the most authentic Italian way (and accent) that it would be best if I could get the oregano from the mountains and the chilli from Michele himself, but that the recipe would still be ok to use if one could not. And to Charleen, who, despite having absolutely no time to do it, still managed to experiment with beans in the Instapot. To Oma, to whom I'm forever indebted for sending me down this path, and who would have never touched an Instapot. To Sasha, who helped me learn more about beans in the vast Indian diet, and topped it off with not one but two vegan recipes that, yes, were made in the Instapot. A thanks to Justin, for always serving the southern staple red beans and rice and being willing to part with the recipe and let us each have a bite. And to Casey for her Tepary Bean Pie invention and willingness to share it with us; my co-workers and I are grateful. As anyone can see just from this small slice of a selection, the Arizona restaurant scene is robustly diverse and full of heart.

I also am indebted to those who have taught me a thing or two about beans over the last few years; some of them may not know it but their work has been instrumental in my own research and increased my love for the humble legume. Steve Sando is the Bean King and I'm proud to have been one of his loyal Bean Club subjects. My pantry is definitely not lacking. Ken Albala's original work in the area of bean history was ahead of its time, as is much of his profoundly well-done research. Gary Nabhan has been a tremendous influence on my own work in all aspects; a huge debt to him is owed for his research, passed along to me for this book, in the areas of beans and agriculture, particularly in the Southwestern u.s. borderlands. Anyone looking to 'eat healthier' should just read Dr Donna M. Winham's extensive studies; her passion for nutrition with regard to beans will set anyone's diet straight. I would have never thought to write for the Edible Series had it not been for accidentally reading a book or study from some of my favourite food scholars: Sidney Mintz, Linda Civitello, Reay Tannahill, Alfred Crosby and Andrew F. Smith, among others. The clear passion they have for their work both amazes and continues to excite me. Of course, to all the bean enthusiasts I've met along this journey – particularly Maya – big thanks to you for standing by the underdogs.

Finally, a particular thank you to Michael Leaman and Andrew F. Smith for their support along the way. Your guidance and patience have been irreplaceable.

Photo Acknowledgements

The author and publishers wish to express their thanks to the below sources of illustrative material and/or permission to reproduce it. Some locations of artworks are also given below, in the interests of brevity:

The American Folklife Center, Library of Congress, Washington, DC: pp. 18, 21 (bottom), 22, 97 (Coal River Folklife Collection, photos Lyntha Scott Eiler), 21 (top), 76 (Paradise Valley Folklife Project Collection, photos Carl Fleischhauer); from Caelius Apicius and Martin Lister, *Apicii Coelii De opsoniis et condimentis sive arte coquinaria* (Amsterdam, 1709): p. 36; Sawyer Bengtson/Unsplash: p. 62; Sneha Chekuri/Unsplash: p. 64; Galleria Colonna, Rome: p. 60; iStock by Getty Images: pp. 6 (rostovtsevayulia), 43 (bhofack2), 63 (IgorDutina), 67 (mauroholanda); from Jacques Le Moyne de Morgues and Theodor de Bry, *Brevis narratio eorvm qvae in Florida Americæ provicia Gallis acciderunt* (Frankfurt am Main, 1591), photo courtesy Getty Research Institute: p. 20; Library of Congress, Prints and Photographs Division, Washington, DC: pp. 23, 91 (photos Carol M. Highsmith Archive), 24 (Marian S. Carson Collection), 28 (collection of David Murray), 48 (photo John Collier, Jr), 56, 57, 59 (Caroline and Erwin Swann Collection), 68, 69, 71 (collection of John Davis Batchelder), 77, 78 (Detroit Publishing Company), 80 (John Margolies Roadside America Photograph Archive), 83 (photo Doris Ulmann), 88 (photo Jack Delano), 93 (Prokudin-Gorskii Collection); Lisovskaya Natalia/

Index

italic numbers refer to illustrations; **bold** to recipes